Bible Promises
to Treasure
for Dad

Bible Promises
to Treasure
for Dad

Inspiring

words

for every

occasion

BROADMAN
&HOLMAN
PUBLISHERS

Nashville, Tennessee

Bible Promises to Treasure for Dads

© 1998 Broadman & Holman Publishers, Nashville, Tennessee

ISBN# 0–633–10050–1

All Scripture passages are from the Authorized King James Version.

******

A note on the sources of quotations. When possible I have
supplied at least the book name from which contemporary quotes
have come. Yet even this is often impossible, since many came
from my "journal of jottings" over many years. Also, if a quote is
from a person who lived longer than fifty or so years ago, I've
made no attempt to cite the source. Such quotations are usually
available in any standard book of quotes.

******

Library of Congress Cataloging-in-Publication Data

Bible promises to treasure for dads

    p. cm.

    Includes bibliographical references.

    ISBN 1–55819–710–9 (hardcover)

        1. Fathers—Religious life—Quotations. 2. Fatherhood—
Religious aspects—Christianity—Quotations, maxims, etc.

    I. Wilde, Gary.

BV4529.P76   1998

248.8'421—dc21

97–23380
CIP

Printed in the United States of America

Contents

Introduction

—One—

Enjoying Your Children   5

Remember that You, Too,
Are Childlike Inside   6
You Are a Child of the New Birth   16
Cherish Your Children   21

—Two—

Loving and Blessing Your Children   24

Love Them by Setting a Good Example   25
Love Them through Training
and Instructing   28
Accept God's Healing for Your
Own Woundedness   31
Bless Your Children, and Envision
Their Future   39

—Three—

Relying on Your Heavenly Father   43

Are You Depending on Others
for Happiness?   44

Are You Feeling Overly Responsible?   45
Are You Able to Say Good-Bye?   46
Discovering Who God Is   49
*Being Encouraged by His Wonderful
Names*   51
Resting in Your Heavenly Father's Care   52
Growing in Trust   58

—Four—

Maintaining a Vibrant Devotional Life   61

Hearing His Word   63
Learning to Pray   64
Offering Praise and Worship   70
Seeking Fellowship   73
Participating in the Lord's Supper   76
Moving into Obedience and Good Works   78

—Five—

Building Your Home upon Godly Values   82

*Be Courageous in Standing
for Biblical Values . . .*   83
Developing Perseverance   86
Growing in Faith   90
Deepening Compassion   92
Putting on Trustworthiness   95
Exercising Humility   98

—Six—
Disciplining with Love   101

Exercise Accountability in Your Own Life   104
*Develop an Atmosphere
of Family Honesty*   105
Teach Obedience to God's Commands   107
Require Respect from Your Children   108
Teach Self-Discipline   110
Look to God for Your Parenting Skills   112
Submission Brings Joy   118

—Seven—
Keeping Your Marriage Strong   120

Remember that God Invented Marriage   121
Do Things that Strengthen a Marriage   123
Follow the Example of a Good Marriage   131
*Recognize the Spiritual Significance
of Marriage*   133

—Eight—
Staying Healthy   136

Maintaining Physical Health   137
Pursuing Emotional Health   140
Learning to Deal with Your Feelings   144
Seeing Yourself as Loved by God   150

—Nine—

Handling Work and Finances Wisely   154

Feeling Worried about Money?   155
Feeling Oppressed at Work?   160
Rest in God's Peace   170

—Ten—

Following Your Biblical Mentors   173

Follow Your Biblical Role Models   174
Abraham: Willingness to Risk for God   175
Noah: Committing to Obedience   178
*Moses: Overcoming Fear
and Low Self-Esteem*   180
*Joshua: Courageously Fighting
Kingdom Battles*   182
Joseph: Learning How to Forgive   185
David: Admitting Mistakes   187
Paul: Pursuing Christian Maturity   190
Jesus: Becoming a Servant-Leader   192

Notes 195

Introduction

I remember as a child singing often at church: "Standing on the Promises of God." Or maybe it was mostly the adults who were singing; but I was standing next to them—my parents and all the others. I recall those faithful people joyfully reciting words they must surely have known by heart . . .

**When the howling storms
of doubt and fear assail,
By the living Word of God I shall prevail,
Standing on the promises of God.**

For years Downey Church, in sunny central Florida, had preached and taught the promises

1

of God and believed in His goodness. From the beginning—when the church building was a small tin-roofed, A-frame at the east end of a dirt road on the outskirts of Orlando—people would gather to stand on the immutable promises. Under the shiny tin roof, standing on the sandy-wooden floorboards, they melded their voices to the tunes of the upright piano and recalled God's goodness. Today, as the church there grows and thrives—now there is also a school and gymnasium—I can only attribute its vibrant life to a love of God's promises and the recognition that without the pledges that flow from the mouth of God, there is no church, no music, and no reason for either.

The promises of God have always been the bedrock of Christian faith; for without God's sacred covenants with us, we cannot survive. In times of joy or heartache, in all our ups and downs, we keep coming back to that source of our life: the motivation for all our doing and the reason for our existence. It is the message of God's mighty assurances: this life is not all there is, He will always be with us while we are here, and He will take us to be with Him someday.

Yes, we do have priceless promises to keep close to our hearts!

My hope for you as you delve into this scriptural treasure chest is that you will grow deeper in love with the One who has spoken as no other ever could. With so many influences bombarding our minds each moment of the day, what could be better than to set aside a few moments of quiet to hear the still, small voice that constantly invites us into warm fellowship? We'll be richly rewarded if we truly listen to what that voice is saying. His words convey blessing and guidance, wisdom and warning, life for now and life everlasting. What incomparable grace!

Gary Wilde
Colorado Springs, 1997

Enjoying Your Children

Do you enjoy your children? If you'd like to enjoy them more, try looking inside yourself for your own childlike qualities. You do have those qualities, but are you allowing them to shine through?

No, we are not called to be "childish." But childlikeness is a valuable characteristic for dads, for God made us with the capacity for enjoying life, just as children are able to do before they learn to be so "proper." The promises in this chapter should help you more fully appreciate the youthful energy of your children. What could be better than having fun with your children, no matter what their age?

Remember that You, Too, Are Childlike Inside

That energy which makes a child hard to manage is the energy which afterward makes him a manager of life.
—Henry Ward Beecher

[Jesus] said, Verily I say unto you, Except ye be converted, and become as little children, ye shall not enter into the kingdom of heaven.
—Matthew 18:3

And now, O LORD my God, thou hast made thy servant king instead of David my father: and I am but a little child: I know not how to go out or come in.

—1 Kings 3:7

Then said I, Ah, Lord GOD! behold, I cannot speak: for I am a child.

But the LORD said unto me, Say not, I am a child: for thou shalt go to all that I shall send thee, and whatsoever I command thee thou shalt speak.

Be not afraid of their faces: for I am with thee to deliver thee, saith the LORD.

—Jeremiah 1:6–8

He shall feed his flock like a shepherd: he shall gather the lambs with his arm, and carry them in his bosom, and shall gently lead those that are with young.

—Isaiah 40:11

Brethren, be not children in understanding: howbeit in malice be ye children, but in understanding be men.

—1 Corinthians 14:20

Whosoever therefore shall humble himself as this little child, the same is greatest in the kingdom of heaven.

—Matthew 18:4

≪ *Take Time for Play*

Thus saith the LORD; I am returned unto Zion, and will dwell in the midst of Jerusalem: and Jerusalem shall be called a city of truth; and the mountain of the LORD of hosts the holy mountain.

Thus saith the LORD of hosts; There shall yet old men and old women dwell in the streets of Jerusalem, and every man with his staff in his hand for very age.

And the streets of the city shall be full of boys and girls playing in the streets thereof.

—Zechariah 8:3–5

And the spirit of the LORD shall rest upon him, the spirit of wisdom and understanding, the spirit of counsel and might, the spirit of knowledge and of the fear of the LORD;

And shall make him of quick understanding in the fear of the LORD: and he shall not judge after the sight of his eyes, neither reprove after the hearing of his ears:

But with righteousness shall he judge the poor, and reprove with equity for the meek of the earth: and he shall smite the earth with the rod of his mouth, and with the breath of his lips shall he slay the wicked.

And righteousness shall be the girdle of his loins, and faithfulness the girdle of his reins.

The wolf also shall dwell with the lamb, and the leopard shall lie down with the kid; and the calf and the young lion and the fatling together; and a little child shall lead them.

And the cow and the bear shall feed; their young ones shall lie down together: and the lion shall eat straw like the ox.

And the sucking child shall play on the hole of the asp, and the weaned child shall put his hand on the cockatrice's den.

They shall not hurt nor destroy in all my holy mountain: for the earth shall be full of the knowledge of the LORD, as the waters cover the sea.

—*Isaiah 11:2–9*

❧ Be Quick to Laugh

Till he fill thy mouth with laughing, and thy lips with rejoicing.

—Job 8:21

Then was our mouth filled with laughter, and our tongue with singing: then said they among the heathen, The LORD hath done great things for them.

—Psalm 126:2

Blessed are ye that hunger now: for ye shall be filled. Blessed are ye that weep now: for ye shall laugh.

—Luke 6:21

❧ Dance with the Little Ones!

They send forth their little ones like a flock, and their children dance.

—Job 21:11

Let them praise his name in the dance: let them sing praises unto him with the timbrel and harp.

—*Psalm 149:3*

[There is] a time to weep, and a time to laugh; a time to mourn, and a time to dance.

—*Ecclesiastes 3:4*

Now Peter and John went up together into the temple at the hour of prayer, being the ninth hour.

And a certain man lame from his mother's womb was carried, whom they laid daily at the gate of the temple which is called Beautiful, to ask alms of them that entered into the temple;

Who seeing Peter and John about to go into the temple asked an alms.

And Peter, fastening his eyes upon him with John, said, Look on us.

And he gave heed unto them, expecting to receive something of them.

Then Peter said, Silver and gold have I none; but such as I have give I thee: In the name of Jesus Christ of Nazareth rise up and walk.

And he took him by the right hand, and lifted him up: and immediately his feet and ankle bones received strength.

And he leaping up stood, and walked, and entered with them into the temple, walking, and leaping, and praising God.

And all the people saw him walking and praising God:

And they knew that it was he which sat for alms at the Beautiful gate of the temple: and they were filled with wonder and amazement at that which had happened unto him.

—Acts 3:1–10

Then shall the lame man leap as an hart, and the tongue of the dumb sing: for in the wilderness shall waters break out, and streams in the desert.

—Isaiah 35:6

⋘ *Be Ready to Sing and Shout*

O come, let us sing unto the LORD: let us make a joyful noise to the rock of our salvation.

Let us come before his presence with thanksgiving, and make a joyful noise unto him with psalms.

For the LORD is a great God, and a great King above all gods.

In his hand are the deep places of the earth: the strength of the hills is his also.

The sea is his, and he made it: and his hands formed the dry land.

O come, let us worship and bow down: let us kneel before the LORD our maker.

For he is our God; and we are the people of his pasture, and the sheep of his hand.

—Psalm 95:1–7a

Make a joyful noise unto the LORD, all ye lands.

Serve the LORD with gladness: come before his presence with singing.

Know ye that the LORD he is God: it is he that hath made us, and not we ourselves; we are his people, and the sheep of his pasture.

Enter into his gates with thanksgiving, and into his courts with praise: be thankful unto him, and bless his name.

For the LORD is good; his mercy is everlasting; and his truth endureth to all generations.

—*Psalm 100*

I will praise thee, O LORD, with my whole heart; I will show forth all thy marvelous works.

I will be glad and rejoice in thee: I will sing praise to thy name, O thou most High.

When mine enemies are turned back, they shall fall and perish at thy presence.

For thou hast maintained my right and my cause; thou satest in the throne judging right.

Thou hast rebuked the heathen, thou hast destroyed the wicked, thou hast put out their name forever and ever.

—*Psalm 9:1–5*

Make a joyful noise unto God, all ye lands:

Sing forth the honor of his name: make his praise glorious.

Say unto God, How terrible art thou in thy works! through the greatness of thy power shall thine enemies submit themselves unto thee.

All the earth shall worship thee, and shall sing unto thee; they shall sing to thy name.

—Psalm 66:1–4

⋘ *Make Joyful Sounds with Your Children*

Rejoice in the LORD, O ye righteous: for praise is comely for the upright.

Praise the LORD with harp: sing unto him with the psaltery and an instrument of ten strings.

Sing unto him a new song; play skillfully with a loud noise.

For the word of the LORD is right; and all his works are done in truth.

He loveth righteousness and judgment: the earth is full of the goodness of the LORD.

—Psalm 33:1–5

Praise him with the sound of the trumpet: praise him with the psaltery and harp.

Praise him with the timbrel and dance: praise him with stringed instruments and organs.

Praise him upon the loud cymbals: praise him upon the high sounding cymbals.

Let every thing that hath breath praise the LORD. Praise ye the LORD.

—*Psalm 150:3–6*

You Are a Child of the New Birth

Seeing God as parent may seem childish. But might there be, in the unadmitted sparkle of the child within you, a sometime longing to climb into God's fatherly lap, to nestle against God's motherly breast, to rest for a moment in the shadow of God's wings or be held in God's strong and tender arms?
If you could allow yourself to feel it, are there not times when you would love to cry on God's shoulder, to let God tell you you are worthwhile and beautiful? And is there not something in you that would be delighted if you could bring a smile to God's face?

—*Gerald May* [1]

Like as a father pitieth his children, so the LORD pitieth them that fear him.

For he knoweth our frame; he remembereth that we are dust.

—*Psalm 103:13–14*

Surely I have behaved and quieted myself, as a child that is weaned of his mother: my soul is even as a weaned child.

—*Psalm 131:2*

Behold, what manner of love the Father hath bestowed upon us, that we should be called the sons of God: therefore the world knoweth us not, because it knew him not.

—*1 John 3:1*

Beloved, now are we the sons of God, and it doth not yet appear what we shall be: but we know that, when he shall appear, we shall be like him; for we shall see him as he is.

And every man that hath this hope in him purifieth himself, even as he is pure.

Whosoever committeth sin transgresseth also the law: for sin is the transgression of the law.

And ye know that he was manifested to take away our sins; and in him is no sin.

Whosoever abideth in him sinneth not: whosoever sinneth hath not seen him, neither known him.

Little children, let no man deceive you: he that doeth righteousness is righteous, even as he is righteous.

He that committeth sin is of the devil; for the devil sinneth from the beginning. For this purpose the Son of God was manifested, that he might destroy the works of the devil.

Whosoever is born of God doth not commit sin; for his seed remaineth in him: and he cannot sin, because he is born of God.

In this the children of God are manifest, and the children of the devil: whosoever doeth not righteousness is not of God, neither he that loveth not his brother.

—1 John 3:2–10

Be ye therefore followers of God, as dear children.

—Ephesians 5:1

There was a man sent from God, whose name was John.

The same came for a witness, to bear witness of the Light, that all men through him might believe.

He was not that Light, but was sent to bear witness of that Light.

That was the true Light, which lighteth every man that cometh into the world.

He was in the world, and the world was made by him, and the world knew him not.

He came unto his own, and his own received him not.

But as many as received him, to them gave he power to become the sons of God, even to them that believe on his name:

—*John 1:6–12*

Marvel not that I said unto thee, Ye must be born again.

The wind bloweth where it listeth, and thou hearest the sound thereof, but canst not tell whence it cometh, and whither it goeth: so is everyone that is born of the Spirit.

Nicodemus answered and said unto him, How can these things be?

Jesus answered and said unto him, Art thou a master of Israel, and knowest not these things?

Verily, verily, I say unto thee, We speak that we do know, and testify that we have seen; and ye receive not our witness.

If I have told you earthly things, and ye believe not, how shall ye believe, if I tell you of heavenly things?

And no man hath ascended up to heaven, but he that came down from heaven, even the Son of man which is in heaven.

And as Moses lifted up the serpent in the wilderness, even so must the Son of man be lifted up:

That whosoever believeth in him should not perish, but have eternal life.

For God so loved the world, that he gave his only begotten Son, that whosoever believeth in him should not perish, but have everlasting life.

—John 3:7–16

Of his own will begat he us with the word of truth, that we should be a kind of firstfruits of his creatures.

—James 1:18

For in him we live, and move, and have our being; as certain also of your own poets have said, For we are also his offspring.

—Acts 17:28

Cherish Your Children

*Most of my childhood memories of my father
are of being ignored. I was his namesake, but
nothing I did ever pleased or even interested
him. He enjoyed telling me I couldn't do
anything right. He had a habit of telling me I
would never amount to anything. He was far
more emotionally destructive than he
realized. I was never rewarded by him with a
comment, a look or a hug. . . . I loved him and
hated him at the same time.*

—*Marlon Brando* [2]

Lo, children are an heritage of the LORD:
and the fruit of the womb is his reward.

As arrows are in the hand of a mighty man;
so are children of the youth.

Happy is the man that hath his quiver full
of them: they shall not be ashamed, but they
shall speak with the enemies in the gate.

—*Psalm 127:3–5*

At the same time came the disciples unto Jesus, saying, Who is the greatest in the kingdom of heaven?

And Jesus called a little child unto him, and set him in the midst of them,

And said, Verily I say unto you, Except ye be converted, and become as little children, ye shall not enter into the kingdom of heaven.

Whosoever therefore shall humble himself as this little child, the same is greatest in the kingdom of heaven.

And whoso shall receive one such little child in my name receiveth me.

But whoso shall offend one of these little ones which believe in me, it were better for him that a millstone were hanged about his neck, and that he were drowned in the depth of the sea.

Woe unto the world because of offences! for it must needs be that offences come; but woe to that man by whom the offence cometh! . . .

Take heed that ye despise not one of these little ones; for I say unto you, That in heaven their angels do always behold the face of my Father which is in heaven.

For the Son of man is come to save that which was lost.

How think ye? if a man have an hundred sheep, and one of them be gone astray, doth he not leave the ninety and nine, and goeth into the mountains, and seeketh that which is gone astray?

And if so be that he find it, verily I say unto you, he rejoiceth more of that sheep, than of the ninety and nine which went not astray.

Even so it is not the will of your Father which is in heaven, that one of these little ones should perish.

—Matthew 18:1–7, 10–14

Loving and Blessing Your Children

Of course, you tell them you love them. But how do they know it? And do they really feel it? Everything we do has an impact on what our children are becoming—especially while they're still at home. They are watching, being men-

tored by us, even when we are not particularly ready to be "on stage." The Scriptures remind us to set the example for our children always and to make sure that their best is uppermost in our minds; for they are a most precious, God-given responsibility.

Love Them by Setting a Good Example

There is nothing more influential in a child's life than the moral power of quiet example. For children to take morality seriously they must see adults take morality seriously.

—William Bennett[1]

Only take heed to thyself, and keep thy soul diligently, lest thou forget the things which thine eyes have seen, and lest they depart from thy heart all the days of thy life: but teach them thy sons, and thy sons' sons;

Specially the day that thou stoodest before the LORD thy God in Horeb, when the LORD said unto me, Gather me the people together, and I will make them hear my words, that they may learn to fear me all the days that they shall live upon the earth, and that they may teach their children.

And ye shall teach them your children, speaking of them when thou sittest in thine house, and when thou walkest by the way, when thou liest down, and when thou risest up.

—*Deuteronomy 4:9–10; 11:19*

There came a man of God unto Eli, and said unto him, Thus saith the LORD, Did I plainly appear unto the house of thy father, when they were in Egypt in Pharaoh's house?

And did I choose him out of all the tribes of Israel to be my priest, to offer upon mine altar, to burn incense, to wear an ephod before me? and did I give unto the house of thy father all the offerings made by fire of the children of Israel?

Wherefore kick ye at my sacrifice and at mine offering, which I have commanded in my habitation; and honorest thy sons above me, to make yourselves fat with the chiefest of all the offerings of Israel my people?

Wherefore the LORD God of Israel saith, I said indeed that thy house, and the house of thy father, should walk before me forever: but now the LORD saith, Be it far from me; for them that honor me I will honor, and they that despise me shall be lightly esteemed.

Behold, the days come, that I will cut off thine arm, and the arm of thy father's house, that there shall not be an old man in thine house.

And thou shalt see an enemy in my habitation, in all the wealth which God shall give Israel: and there shall not be an old man in thine house forever.

And the man of thine, whom I shall not cut off from mine altar, shall be to consume thine eyes, and to grieve thine heart: and all the increase of thine house shall die in the flower of their age.

And this shall be a sign unto thee, that shall come upon thy two sons, on Hophni and Phinehas; in one day they shall die both of them.

—*1 Samuel 2:27–34*

Ye shall not afflict any widow, or fatherless child.

If thou afflict them in any wise, and they
cry at all unto me, I will surely hear their cry.
—*Exodus 22:22–23*

Love Them through Training and Instructing

*Parents must not cowardly abdicate their
authority. Youths who win their
independence too easily, without having had
to wrest it from their resisting parents, are
very poorly prepared to make use of it in life.
In the struggle the child will acquire
experience; he will learn how far he may resist
and at what point he must submit.*

—*Paul Tournier*[2]

Train up a child in the way he should go:
and when he is old, he will not depart from it.
—*Proverbs 22:6*

For I know him, that he will command his children and his household after him, and they shall keep the way of the LORD, to do justice and judgment.

—*Genesis 18:19a*

And thou shalt show thy son in that day, saying, This is done because of that which the LORD did unto me when I came forth out of Egypt.

—*Exodus 13:8*

Correct thy son, and he shall give thee rest; yea, he shall give delight unto thy soul.

—*Proverbs 29:17*

Give ear, O my people, to my law: incline your ears to the words of my mouth.

I will open my mouth in a parable: I will utter dark sayings of old:

Which we have heard and known, and our fathers have told us.

We will not hide them from their children, showing to the generation to come the praises of the LORD, and his strength, and his wonderful works that he hath done.

For he established a testimony in Jacob, and appointed a law in Israel, which he commanded our fathers, that they should make them known to their children:

That the generation to come might know them, even the children which should be born; who should arise and declare them to their children:

That they might set their hope in God, and not forget the works of God, but keep his commandments:

And might not be as their fathers, a stubborn and rebellious generation; a generation that set not their heart aright, and whose spirit was not steadfast with God.

—Psalms 78:1–8

These words, which I command thee this day, shall be in thine heart:

And thou shalt teach them diligently unto thy children, and shalt talk of them when thou sittest in thine house, and when thou walkest by the way, and when thou liest down, and when thou risest up.

And thou shalt bind them for a sign upon thine hand, and they shall be as frontlets between thine eyes.

And thou shalt write them upon the posts of thy house, and on thy gates.

—Deuteronomy 6:6–9

And, ye fathers, provoke not your children to wrath: but bring them up in the nurture and admonition of the Lord.

—Ephesians 6:4

Accept God's Healing for Your Own Woundedness

The caliber of divine love eludes us mortals. We are, for the most part, so selfish, so self-centered, so self-preoccupied, we recoil from those spike-torn hands extended to us in mercy, compassion and deep longing. We simply refuse to believe anyone truly can care for us with such pure motives.

—W. Phillip Keller[3]

The LORD is my shepherd; I shall not want. He maketh me to lie down in green pastures: he leadeth me beside the still waters.

He restoreth my soul: he leadeth me in the paths of righteousness for his name's sake.

Yea, though I walk through the valley of the shadow of death, I will fear no evil: for thou art with me; thy rod and thy staff they comfort me.

Thou preparest a table before me in the presence of mine enemies: thou anointest my head with oil; my cup runneth over.

Surely goodness and mercy shall follow me all the days of my life: and I will dwell in the house of the LORD forever.

—Psalm 23

Praise ye the LORD: for it is good to sing praises unto our God; for it is pleasant; and praise is comely.

The LORD doth build up Jerusalem: he gathereth together the outcasts of Israel.

He healeth the broken in heart, and bindeth up their wounds.

—Psalm 147:1–3

For he maketh sore, and bindeth up: he woundeth, and his hands make whole.

Job 5:18

◂◂ *Forgive Past Abusive Relationships*

For if ye forgive men their trespasses, your heavenly Father will also forgive you:

But if ye forgive not men their trespasses, neither will your Father forgive your trespasses.

—Matthew 6:14–15

So shall ye say unto Joseph, Forgive, I pray thee now, the trespass of thy brethren, and their sin; for they did unto thee evil: and now, we pray thee, forgive the trespass of the servants of the God of thy father. And Joseph wept when they spake unto him.

And his brethren also went and fell down before his face; and they said, Behold, we be thy servants.

And Joseph said unto them, Fear not: for am I in the place of God?

But as for you, ye thought evil against me; but God meant it unto good, . . .

Now therefore fear ye not: I will nourish you, and your little ones. And he comforted them, and spake kindly unto them.

—Genesis 50:17–20a, 21

Then came Peter to him, and said, Lord, how oft shall my brother sin against me, and I forgive him? till seven times?

Jesus saith unto him, I say not unto thee, Until seven times: but, Until seventy times seven. . . .

Shouldest not thou also have had compassion on thy fellow servant, even as I had pity on thee?

—Matthew 18:21–22, 33

For this is thankworthy, if a man for conscience toward God endure grief, suffering wrongfully.

For what glory is it, if, when ye be buffeted for your faults, ye shall take it patiently? but if, when ye do well, and suffer for it, ye take it patiently, this is acceptable with God.

For even hereunto were ye called: because Christ also suffered for us, leaving us an example, that ye should follow his steps:

Who did no sin, neither was guile found in his mouth:

Who, when he was reviled, reviled not again; when he suffered, he threatened not; but committed himself to him that judgeth righteously.

—1 Peter 2:19–23

Let this mind be in you, which was also in Christ Jesus:

Who, being in the form of God, thought it not robbery to be equal with God:

But made himself of no reputation, and took upon him the form of a servant, and was made in the likeness of men:

And being found in fashion as a man, he humbled himself, and became obedient unto death, even the death of the cross.

Wherefore God also hath highly exalted him, and given him a name which is above every name:

That at the name of Jesus every knee should bow, of things in heaven, and things in earth, and things under the earth;

And that every tongue should confess that Jesus Christ is Lord, to the glory of God the Father.

—*Philippians 2:5–11*

⋘ *Break Free of the Heritage of Parental Sins*

Yet say ye, Why? doth not the son bear the iniquity of the father? When the son hath done that which is lawful and right, and hath kept all my statutes, and hath done them, he shall surely live.

The soul that sinneth, it shall die. The son shall not bear the iniquity of the father, neither shall the father bear the iniquity of the son: the righteousness of the righteous shall be upon him, and the wickedness of the wicked shall be upon him.

But if the wicked will turn from all his sins that he hath committed, and keep all my statutes, and do that which is lawful and right, he shall surely live, he shall not die.

All his transgressions that he hath committed, they shall not be mentioned unto him: in his righteousness that he hath done he shall live.

Have I any pleasure at all that the wicked should die? saith the Lord GOD: and not that he should return from his ways, and live?

But when the righteous turneth away from his righteousness, and committeth iniquity, and doeth according to all the abominations that the wicked man doeth, shall he live? All his righteousness that he hath done shall not be mentioned: in his trespass that he hath trespassed, and in his sin that he hath sinned, in them shall he die.

Yet ye say, The way of the Lord is not equal. Hear now, O house of Israel; Is not my way equal? are not your ways unequal?

When a righteous man turneth away from his righteousness, and committeth iniquity, and dieth in them; for his iniquity that he hath done shall he die.

Again, when the wicked man turneth away from his wickedness that he hath committed, and doeth that which is lawful and right, he shall save his soul alive.

Because he considereth, and turneth away from all his transgressions that he hath committed, he shall surely live, he shall not die.

Yet saith the house of Israel, The way of the Lord is not equal. O house of Israel, are not my ways equal? are not your ways unequal?

Therefore I will judge you, O house of Israel, everyone according to his ways, saith the Lord GOD. Repent, and turn yourselves from all your transgressions; so iniquity shall not be your ruin.

Cast away from you all your transgressions, whereby ye have transgressed; and make you a new heart and a new spirit: for why will ye die, O house of Israel?

For I have no pleasure in the death of him that dieth, saith the Lord GOD: wherefore turn yourselves, and live ye.

—*Ezekiel 18:19–32*

Bless Your Children, and Envision Their Future

When I approach a child,
he inspires in me two sentiments:
tenderness for what he is,
and respect for what he may become.
—Louis Pasteur

And God blessed them, saying, Be fruitful, and multiply, and fill the waters in the seas, and let fowl multiply in the earth.

—*Genesis 1:22*

And his father Isaac said unto him, Come near now, and kiss me, my son.

And he came near, and kissed him: and he smelled the smell of his raiment, and blessed him, and said, See, the smell of my son is as the smell of a field which the LORD hath blessed:

Therefore God give thee of the dew of heaven, and the fatness of the earth, and plenty of corn and wine:

Let people serve thee, and nations bow down to thee: be lord over thy brethren, and

let thy mother's sons bow down to thee:
cursed be everyone that curseth thee, and
blessed be he that blesseth thee.

—Genesis 27:26–29

Israel beheld Joseph's sons, and said, Who
are these?

And Joseph said unto his father, They are
my sons, whom God hath given me in this
place. And he said, Bring them, I pray thee,
unto me, and I will bless them.

Now the eyes of Israel were dim for age, so
that he could not see. And he brought them
near unto him; and he kissed them, and
embraced them.

And Israel said unto Joseph, I had not
thought to see thy face: and, lo, God hath
showed me also thy seed.

And Joseph brought them out from
between his knees, and he bowed himself with
his face to the earth.

And Joseph took them both, Ephraim in
his right hand toward Israel's left hand, and
Manasseh in his left hand toward Israel's right
hand, and brought them near unto him.

And Israel stretched out his right hand, and laid it upon Ephraim's head, who was the younger, and his left hand upon Manasseh's head, guiding his hands wittingly; for Manasseh was the firstborn.

And he blessed Joseph, and said, God, before whom my fathers Abraham and Isaac did walk, the God which fed me all my life long unto this day,

The Angel which redeemed me from all evil, bless the lads; and let my name be named on them, and the name of my fathers Abraham and Isaac; and let them grow into a multitude in the midst of the earth.

—Genesis 48:8–16

Speak unto Aaron and unto his sons, saying, On this wise ye shall bless the children of Israel, saying unto them,

The LORD bless thee, and keep thee:

The LORD make his face shine upon thee, and be gracious unto thee:

The LORD lift up his countenance upon thee, and give thee peace.

—Numbers 6:23–26

Naomi said unto her two daughters-in-law, Go, return each to her mother's house: the LORD deal kindly with you, as ye have dealt with the dead, and with me.

The LORD grant you that ye may find rest, each of you in the house of her husband. Then she kissed them; and they lifted up their voice, and wept.

—*Ruth 1:8–9*

He led them out as far as to Bethany, and he lifted up his hands, and blessed them.

And it came to pass, while he blessed them, he was parted from them, and carried up into heaven.

And they worshiped him, and returned to Jerusalem with great joy:

And were continually in the temple, praising and blessing God. Amen.

—*Luke 24:50–53*

Relying on Your Heavenly Father

It's tempting to take all the credit for the things that happen to us—whether we view them as good or bad. But Another is at work in our lives!

If we are children of our heavenly Father, everything that takes place in our days proceeds through His "office" and is marked "Approved." Although He doesn't necessarily cause everything that happens, He certainly allows it. And His promise is this: to be with us in every circumstance, providing comfort, care, and strength to endure every trial. He is a Lord to rely on.

Are You Depending on Others for Happiness?

God, who has made us, knows what we are and that our happiness lies in him. Yet we will not seek it in him as long as he leaves us any other resort where it can even plausibly be looked for. While what we call "our own life" remains agreeable we will not surrender it to him.

—C.S. Lewis[1]

All flesh is grass, and all the goodliness thereof is as the flower of the field:

The grass withereth, the flower fadeth: because the spirit of the LORD bloweth upon it: surely the people is grass.

—Isaiah 40:6b–7

Remember now thy Creator in the days of thy youth, while the evil days come not, nor the years draw nigh, when thou shalt say, I have no pleasure in them.

—*Ecclesiastes 12:1*

Are You Feeling Overly Responsible?

I have a new philosophy.
I'm only going to dread one day at a time.
—*Charlie Brown (Charles Schultz)*

Now it came to pass, as they went, that he entered into a certain village: and a certain woman named Martha received him into her house.

And she had a sister called Mary, which also sat at Jesus' feet, and heard his word.

But Martha was cumbered about much serving, and came to him, and said, Lord, dost thou not care that my sister hath left me to serve alone? bid her therefore that she help me.

And Jesus answered and said unto her, Martha, Martha, thou art careful and troubled about many things:

But one thing is needful: and Mary hath chosen that good part, which shall not be taken away from her.

—Luke 10:38–42

Are You Able to Say Good-Bye?

God brings into our lives the loss of what we have been holding onto, what identifies us, what is "saving" our ego. We are forced to let it go and given the opportunity to just be in His love.

—Gerald May[2]

≪ Departing from Father and Mother

And the LORD God caused a deep sleep to fall upon Adam, and he slept: and he took one of his ribs, and closed up the flesh instead thereof;

And the rib, which the LORD God had taken from man, made he a woman, and brought her unto the man.

And Adam said, This is now bone of my bones, and flesh of my flesh: she shall be called Woman, because she was taken out of Man.

Therefore shall a man leave his father and his mother, and shall cleave unto his wife: and they shall be one flesh.

—Genesis 2:21–24

⋘ "Leaving" Home and Family of Origin . . .

And it came to pass, that, as they went in the way, a certain man said unto him, Lord, I will follow thee whithersoever thou goest.

And Jesus said unto him, Foxes have holes, and birds of the air have nests; but the Son of man hath not where to lay his head.

And he said unto another, Follow me. But he said, Lord, suffer me first to go and bury my father.

Jesus said unto him, Let the dead bury their dead: but go thou and preach the kingdom of God.

—Luke 9:57–60

⋘ . . . To Follow Christ

Then said he unto him, A certain man made a great supper, and bade many:

And sent his servant at supper time to say to them that were bidden, Come; for all things are now ready.

And they all with one consent began to make excuse. The first said unto him, I have bought a piece of ground, and I must needs go and see it: I pray thee have me excused.

And another said, I have bought five yoke of oxen, and I go to prove them: I pray thee have me excused.

And another said, I have married a wife, and therefore I cannot come.

So that servant came, and showed his lord these things. Then the master of the house being angry said to his servant, Go out quickly into the streets and lanes of the city, and bring in hither the poor, and the maimed, and the halt, and the blind.

And the servant said, Lord, it is done as thou hast commanded, and yet there is room.

And the lord said unto the servant, Go out into the highways and hedges, and compel them to come in, that my house may be filled.

For I say unto you, That none of those men which were bidden shall taste of my supper. . . . and he turned, and said unto them,

If any man come to me, and hate not his father, and mother, and wife, and children, and brethren, and sisters, yea, and his own life also, he cannot be my disciple.

—*Luke 14:16–24, 25b–26*

Discovering Who God Is

Give us
A pure heart
That we may see thee,
A humble heart
That we may hear thee,
A heart of love
that we may serve thee,
Thou
Whom I do not know
But whose I am.

—*Dag Hammarskjold*[3]

Be still, and know that I am God: I will be exalted among the heathen, I will be exalted in the earth.

—*Psalm 46:10*

Then Paul stood in the midst of Mars' hill, and said, Ye men of Athens, I perceive that in all things ye are too superstitious.

For as I passed by, and beheld your devotions, I found an altar with this inscription, TO THE UNKNOWN GOD. Whom therefore ye ignorantly worship, him declare I unto you.

God that made the world and all things therein, seeing that he is Lord of heaven and earth, dwelleth not in temples made with hands;

Neither is worshiped with men's hands, as though he needed anything, seeing he giveth to all life and breath, and all things;

And hath made of one blood all nations ofmen for to dwell on all the face of the earth, and hath determined the times before appointed, and the bounds of their habitation;

That they should seek the Lord, if haply they might feel after him, and find him, though he be not far from every one of us.

—Acts 17:22–27

Being Encouraged by His Wonderful Names

❧ *The Lord Is Present with Me*

It was round about eighteen thousand measures: and the name of the city from that day shall be, The LORD is there.

—*Ezekiel 48:35*

❧ *The Lord Makes Holy*

Speak thou also unto the children of Israel, saying, Verily my sabbaths ye shall keep: for it is a sign between me and you throughout your generations; that ye may know that I am the LORD that doth sanctify you.

—*Exodus 31:13*

❧ *The Lord Heals*

If thou wilt diligently hearken to the voice of the LORD thy God, and wilt do that which is right in his sight, and wilt give ear to his commandments, and keep all his statutes, I will put none of these diseases upon thee, which I have brought upon the Egyptians: for I am the LORD that healeth thee.

—*Exodus 15:26*

⋘ *The Lord Is Our Righteousness*

In his days Judah shall be saved, and Israel shall dwell safely: and this is his name whereby he shall be called, THE LORD OUR RIGHTEOUSNESS.

—*Jeremiah 23:6*

Resting in Your Heavenly Father's Care

To live content with small means;
To seek elegance rather than luxury,
and refinement rather than fashion;
To be worthy, not respectable,
and wealthy, not rich;
To study hard, think quietly, talk gently.
To listen to stars and birds,

to babes and sages, with open heart;
To bear all cheerfully, do all bravely,
await occasion, hurry never;
In a word, to let the spiritual, unbidden and
unconscious, grow up through the common:
This is to be my symphony.

—*William Ellery Channing*

But whoso hearkeneth unto me shall dwell safely, and shall be quiet from fear of evil.

—*Proverbs 1:33*

Stand fast therefore in the liberty wherewith Christ hath made us free, and be not entangled again with the yoke of bondage.

—*Galatians 5:1*

Take therefore no thought for the morrow: for the morrow shall take thought for the things of itself. Sufficient unto the day is the evil thereof.

—*Matthew 6:34*

Who is a God like unto thee, that pardoneth iniquity, and passeth by the transgression of the remnant of his heritage? he retaineth not his anger forever, because he delighteth in mercy.

He will turn again, he will have compassion upon us; he will subdue our iniquities; and thou wilt cast all their sins into the depths of the sea.

—*Micah 7:18–19*

Having therefore, brethren, boldness to enter into the holiest by the blood of Jesus,

By a new and living way, which he hath consecrated for us, through the veil, that is to say, his flesh;

And having an high priest over the house of God;

Let us draw near with a true heart in full assurance of faith, having our hearts sprinkled from an evil conscience, and our bodies washed with pure water.

—*Hebrews 10:19–22*

Now unto him that is able to do exceeding abundantly above all that we ask or think, according to the power that worketh in us.

—Ephesians 3:20

⋘ *Live by His Spirit*

And I will pray the Father, and he shall give you another Comforter, that he may abide with you forever;

Even the Spirit of truth; whom the world cannot receive, because it seeth him not, neither knoweth him: but ye know him; for he dwelleth with you, and shall be in you. . . .

But the Comforter, which is the Holy Ghost, whom the Father will send in my name, he shall teach you all things, and bring all things to your remembrance, whatsoever I have said unto you.

Peace I leave with you, my peace I give unto you: not as the world giveth, give I unto you. Let not your heart be troubled, neither let it be afraid.

—John 14:16–17, 26–27

⋘ *Walk in His Strength*

When thou goest, thy steps shall not be straitened; and when thou runnest, thou shalt not stumble.

—Proverbs 4:12

For by thee I have run through a troop: by my God have I leaped over a wall.

—2 Samuel 22:30

He giveth power to the faint; and to them that have no might he increaseth strength.

Even the youths shall faint and be weary, and the young men shall utterly fall:

But they that wait upon the LORD shall renew their strength; they shall mount up with wings as eagles; they shall run, and not be weary; and they shall walk, and not faint.

—Isaiah 40:29–31

Lay not up for yourselves treasures upon earth, where moth and rust doth corrupt, and where thieves break through and steal:

But lay up for yourselves treasures in heaven, where neither moth nor rust doth corrupt, and where thieves do not break through nor steal:

For where your treasure is, there will your heart be also.

—Matthew 6:19–21

O God, thou art my God; early will I seek thee: my soul thirsteth for thee, my flesh longeth for thee in a dry and thirsty land, where no water is.

—Psalm 63:1

Ask, and it shall be given you; seek, and ye shall find; knock, and it shall be opened unto you.

—Matthew 7:7

Growing in Trust

O Lord, sea of love and goodness,
let me not fear too much the storms and winds
of my daily life,
and let me know that there is
ebb and flow
but that the sea remains the sea.

—*Henri Nouwen*[4]

God is our refuge and strength, a very present help in trouble.

Therefore will not we fear, though the earth be removed, and though the mountains be carried into the midst of the sea;

Though the waters thereof roar and be troubled, though the mountains shake with the swelling thereof. . . .

The LORD of hosts is with us; the God of Jacob is our refuge.

—*Psalm 46:1–3, 7*

Therefore I say unto you, Take no thought for your life, what ye shall eat, or what ye shall drink; nor yet for your body, what ye shall put on. Is not the life more than meat, and the body than raiment?

Behold the fowls of the air: for they sow not, neither do they reap, nor gather into barns; yet your heavenly Father feedeth them. Are ye not much better than they?

Which of you by taking thought can add one cubit unto his stature?

And why take ye thought for raiment? Consider the lilies of the field, how they grow; they toil not, neither do they spin:

And yet I say unto you, That even Solomon in all his glory was not arrayed like one of these.

Wherefore, if God so clothe the grass of the field, which today is, and tomorrow is cast into the oven, shall he not much more clothe you, O ye of little faith?

Therefore take no thought, saying, What shall we eat? or, What shall we drink? or, Wherewithal shall we be clothed?

(For after all these things do the Gentiles seek:) for your heavenly Father knoweth that ye have need of all these things.

But seek ye first the kingdom of God, and his righteousness; and all these things shall be added unto you.

—*Matthew 6:25–33*

Be careful for nothing; but in everything by prayer and supplication with thanksgiving let your requests be made known unto God.

And the peace of God, which passeth all understanding, shall keep your hearts and minds through Christ Jesus.

—Philippians 4:6–7

I can do all things through Christ which strengtheneth me.

—Philippians 4:13

Four

Maintaining a Vibrant Devotional Life

❧

"There's just never enough time for everything that needs to be done!" said Jerry, after a long day some months ago. It had been that way at work, and it was the same at home, especially when he tried to carve out a little time for the Lord.

But then Jerry began to see that "everything" could come next—after his devotional life—and, gradually, after adjusting his priorities over the weeks, he began to see something even more significant about his spiritual life: it was happening all the time. His spiritual life was more than the little bits of time he carved out for his quiet time. He began to sense God's presence in all of his endeavors. And the things he did— reading the Word, praying, and enjoying fellowship in the church—only strengthened His love and desire for that blessed Presence.

Hearing His Word

Lord, as I read . . .
let me hear you singing.
As I read your words,
let me hear you speaking.
As I reflect on each page,
let me see your image.
And as I seek to put your precepts into practice,
let my heart be filled with joy.

—*Lady Jane Grey*

All scripture is given by inspiration of God, and is profitable for doctrine, for reproof, for correction, for instruction in righteousness:

That the man of God may be perfect, thoroughly furnished unto all good works.

—*2 Timothy 3:16–17*

Thy word have I hid in mine heart, that I might not sin against thee. . . .

I will delight myself in thy statutes: I will not forget thy word. . . .

So shall I have wherewith to answer him that reproacheth me: for I trust in thy word. . . .

This is my comfort in my affliction: for thy word hath quickened me.

—Psalm 119:11, 16, 42, 50

For the word of God is quick, and powerful, and sharper than any two-edged sword, piercing even to the dividing asunder of soul and spirit, and of the joints and marrow, and is a discerner of the thoughts and intents of the heart.

Neither is there any creature that is not manifest in his sight: but all things are naked and opened unto the eyes of him with whom we have to do.

—Hebrews 4:12–13

Learning to Pray

More things are wrought by prayer
Than this world dreams of.
Wherefore, let thy voice
Rise like a fountain for me night and day.
For what are men better than sheep or goats
That nourish a blind life within the brain,
If, knowing God, they lift not hands of prayer
Both for themselves and those
who call them friends?

—Alfred Lord Tennyson

It shall come to pass, that before they call, I will answer; and while they are yet speaking, I will hear.

—*Isaiah 65:24*

When thou prayest, thou shalt not be as the hypocrites are: for they love to pray standing in the synagogues and in the corners of the streets, that they may be seen of men. Verily I say unto you, They have their reward.

But thou, when thou prayest, enter into thy closet, and when thou hast shut thy door, pray to thy Father which is in secret; and thy Father which seeth in secret shall reward thee openly.

But when ye pray, use not vain repetitions, as the heathen do: for they think that they shall be heard for their much speaking.

Be not ye therefore like unto them: for your Father knoweth what things ye have need of, before ye ask him.

After this manner therefore pray ye: Our Father which art in heaven, Hallowed be thy name.

Thy kingdom come. Thy will be done in earth, as it is in heaven.

Give us this day our daily bread.

And forgive us our debts, as we forgive our debtors.

And lead us not into temptation, but deliver us from evil: For thine is the kingdom, and the power, and the glory, forever.

—Matthew 6:5–13

These things have I written unto you that believe on the name of the Son of God; that ye may know that ye have eternal life, and that ye may believe on the name of the Son of God.

And this is the confidence that we have in him, that, if we ask any thing according to his will, he heareth us:

And if we know that he hear us, whatsoever we ask, we know that we have the petitions that we desired of him.

—1 John 5:13–15

Ask, and it shall be given you; seek, and ye shall find; knock, and it shall be opened unto you:

For everyone that asketh receiveth; and he that seeketh findeth; and to him that knock-eth it shall be opened.

Or what man is there of you, whom if his son ask bread, will he give him a stone?

Or if he ask a fish, will he give him a serpent?

If ye then, being evil, know how to give good gifts unto your children, how much more shall your Father which is in heaven give good things to them that ask him?

—*Matthew 7:7–11*

Is any among you afflicted? let him pray. Is any merry? let him sing psalms.

Is any sick among you? let him call for the elders of the church; and let them pray over him, anointing him with oil in the name of the Lord:

And the prayer of faith shall save the sick, and the Lord shall raise him up; and if he have committed sins, they shall be forgiven him.

Confess your faults one to another, and pray one for another, that ye may be healed. The effectual fervent prayer of a righteous man availeth much.

Elijah was a man subject to like passions as we are, and he prayed earnestly that it might not rain: and it rained not on the earth by the space of three years and six months.

And he prayed again, and the heaven gave rain, and the earth brought forth her fruit.

—*James 5:13–18*

Let us draw near with a true heart in full assurance of faith, having our hearts sprinkled from an evil conscience, and our bodies washed with pure water.

—*Hebrews 10:22*

For we are saved by hope: but hope that is seen is not hope: for what a man seeth, why doth he yet hope for?

But if we hope for that we see not, then do we with patience wait for it.

Likewise the Spirit also helpeth our infirmities: for we know not what we should pray for as we ought: but the Spirit itself maketh intercession for us with groanings which cannot be uttered.

And he that searcheth the hearts knoweth what is the mind of the Spirit, because he maketh intercession for the saints according to the will of God.

And we know that all things work together for good to them that love God, to them who are the called according to his purpose.

—*Romans 8:24–28*

Let us therefore come boldly unto the throne of grace, that we may obtain mercy, and find grace to help in time of need.

—*Hebrews 4:16*

And whatsoever we ask, we receive of him, because we keep his commandments, and do those things that are pleasing in his sight.

—*1 John 3:22*

Offering Praise and Worship

Be a gardener.
Dig a ditch, toil and sweat,
and turn the earth upside down
and seek the deepness
and water the plants in time.
Continue this labor
and make sweet floods to run
and noble and abundant fruits to spring.
Take this food and drink
and carry it to God
as your true worship.

—Julian of Norwich

O come, let us worship and bow down: let us kneel before the LORD our maker.

—Psalm 95:6

This is the day which the LORD hath made; we will rejoice and be glad in it.

—Psalm 118:24

Praise ye the LORD. Praise God in his sanctuary: praise him in the firmament of his power.

Praise him for his mighty acts: praise him according to his excellent greatness.

Praise him with the sound of the trumpet: praise him with the psaltery and harp.

Praise him with the timbrel and dance: praise him with stringed instruments and organs.

Praise him upon the loud cymbals: praise him upon the high sounding cymbals.

Let every thing that hath breath praise the LORD. Praise ye the LORD.

—*Psalm 150*

Then saith Jesus unto him, Get thee hence, Satan: for it is written, Thou shalt worship the Lord thy God, and him only shalt thou serve.

—*Matthew 4:10*

Jesus saith unto her, Woman, believe me, the hour cometh, when ye shall neither in this mountain, nor yet at Jerusalem, worship the Father.

Ye worship ye know not what: we know what we worship: for salvation is of the Jews.

71

But the hour cometh, and now is, when the true worshipers shall worship the Father in spirit and in truth: for the Father seeketh such to worship him.

God is a Spirit: and they that worship him must worship him in spirit and in truth.

—*John 4:21–24*

Let the word of Christ dwell in you richly in all wisdom; teaching and admonishing one another in psalms and hymns and spiritual songs, singing with grace in your hearts to the Lord.

—*Colossians 3:16*

Seeking Fellowship

Not what a man is in himself as a Christian, his spirituality and piety, constitutes the basis of our community. What determines our brotherhood is what that man is by reason of Christ. Our community with one another consists solely in what Christ has done to both of us. This is true not merely at the beginning . . . it remains so for all the future and to all eternity.

—*Dietrich Bonhoeffer[1]*

Behold, how good and how pleasant it is for brethren to dwell together in unity!

It is like the precious ointment upon the head, that ran down upon the beard, even Aaron's beard: that went down to the skirts of his garments;

As the dew of Hermon, and as the dew that descended upon the mountains of Zion: for there the LORD commanded the blessing, even life for evermore.

—*Psalm 133*

And they continued steadfastly in the apostles' doctrine and fellowship, and in breaking of bread, and in prayers.

And fear came upon every soul: and many wonders and signs were done by the apostles.

And all that believed were together, and had all things common;

And sold their possessions and goods, and parted them to all men, as every man had need.

And they, continuing daily with one accord in the temple, and breaking bread from house to house, did eat their meat with gladness and singleness of heart,

Praising God, and having favor with all the people. And the Lord added to the church daily such as should be saved.

—Acts 2:42–47

Be kindly affectioned one to another with brotherly love; in honor preferring one another.

—Romans 12:10

Not forsaking the assembling of ourselves together, as the manner of some is; but exhorting one another: and so much the more, as ye see the day approaching.

—*Hebrews 10:25*

He that saith he is in the light, and hateth his brother, is in darkness even until now.

He that loveth his brother abideth in the light, and there is none occasion of stumbling in him.

But he that hateth his brother is in darkness, and walketh in darkness, and knoweth not whither he goeth, because that darkness hath blinded his eyes.

—*1 John 2:9–11*

Participating in the Lord's Supper

As I take the bread and the cup, I find new strength and increased vigor coming into my life. With the bread, I look back in penitence and thank Him for His forgiveness. With the cup, I look forward and thank Him for His promise of strength for whatever comes. As I rise from this place, let me set out anew to follow Him wherever He leads.

—*E. Paul Hovey*[2]

As they were eating, Jesus took bread, and blessed it, and brake it, and gave it to the disciples, and said, Take, eat; this is my body.

And he took the cup, and gave thanks, and gave it to them, saying, Drink ye all of it;

For this is my blood of the new testament, which is shed for many for the remission of sins.

—*Matthew 26:26–28*

For I have received of the Lord that which also I delivered unto you, That the Lord Jesus the same night in which he was betrayed took bread:

And when he had given thanks, he brake it, and said, Take, eat: this is my body, which is broken for you: this do in remembrance of me.

After the same manner also he took the cup, when he had supped, saying, This cup is the new testament in my blood: this do ye, as oft as ye drink it, in remembrance of me.

For as often as ye eat this bread, and drink this cup, ye do show the Lord's death till he come.

—*1 Corinthians 11:23–26*

Wherefore whosoever shall eat this bread, and drink this cup of the Lord, unworthily, shall be guilty of the body and blood of the Lord.

But let a man examine himself, and so let him eat of that bread, and drink of that cup.

For he that eateth and drinketh unworthily, eateth and drinketh damnation to himself, not discerning the Lord's body.

For this cause many are weak and sickly among you, and many sleep.

—*1 Corinthians 11:27–30*

Moving into Obedience and Good Works

Do all the good you can,
By all the means you can,
In all the ways you can,
In all the places you can,
At all the times you can,
To all the people you can,
As long as ever you can.

—John Wesley

And whatsoever ye do in word or deed, do all in the name of the Lord Jesus, giving thanks to God and the Father by him.

—*Colossians 3:17*

But what think ye? A certain man had two sons; and he came to the first, and said, Son, go work today in my vineyard.

He answered and said, I will not: but afterward he repented, and went.

And he came to the second, and said likewise. And he answered and said, I go, sir: and went not.

Whether of them twain did the will of his father? They say unto him, The first. Jesus saith unto them, Verily I say unto you, That the publicans and the harlots go into the kingdom of God before you.

—Matthew 21:28–31

For by grace are ye saved through faith; and that not of yourselves: it is the gift of God:

Not of works, lest any man should boast.

For we are his workmanship, created in Christ Jesus unto good works, which God hath before ordained that we should walk in them.

—Ephesians 2:8–10

For to me to live is Christ, and to die is gain.

—Philippians 1:21

If ye then be risen with Christ, seek those things which are above, where Christ sitteth on the right hand of God.

Set your affection on things above, not on things on the earth.

For ye are dead, and your life is hid with Christ in God.

When Christ, who is our life, shall appear, then shall ye also appear with him in glory.

Mortify therefore your members which are upon the earth; fornication, uncleanness, inordinate affection, evil concupiscence, and covetousness, which is idolatry:

For which things' sake the wrath of God cometh on the children of disobedience:

In the which ye also walked some time, when ye lived in them.

But now ye also put off all these; anger, wrath, malice, blasphemy, filthy communication out of your mouth.

Lie not one to another, seeing that ye have put off the old man with his deeds.

—*Colossians 3:1–9*

Wherefore lay apart all filthiness and superfluity of naughtiness, and receive with meekness the engrafted word, which is able to save your souls.

But be ye doers of the word, and not hearers only, deceiving your own selves.

For if any be a hearer of the word, and not a doer, he is like unto a man beholding his natural face in a glass:

For he beholdeth himself, and goeth his way, and straightway forgetteth what manner of man he was.

But whoso looketh into the perfect law of liberty, and continueth therein, he being not a forgetful hearer, but a doer of the work, this man shall be blessed in his deed.

If any man among you seem to be religious, and bridleth not his tongue, but deceiveth his own heart, this man's religion is vain.

Pure religion and undefiled before God and the Father is this, To visit the fatherless and widows in their affliction, and to keep himself unspotted from the world.

—*James 1:21–27*

Five

Building Your Home upon Godly Values

❧

*T*oday we are inundated by various worldviews and the values that flow from them. Some say that we should, in the name of tolerance, accept all value systems as equal and that we must not attempt to distinguish between a "good" and a "bad" point of view. Sincerity is the key, the ultimate value.

In the face of this call to relativism, the clear command of Scripture rings out: "Do not be conformed to this world." We must acknowledge the moral absolutes; indeed, since our universe is the product of a moral Creator, we could not live without them.

Be Courageous in Standing for Biblical Values . . .

Moral courage is great and admirable in itself; but it must be pointed out that it almost never appears except as part of that greater entity called character.

A man without character may give fitful exhibitions of courage . . . but no man without character is consistently courageous, just as no man of real character is lacking in consistent courage. In short, moral courage is allied with other traits which make up character: honesty, deep seriousness, a firm sense of principle, candor, resolution.

—*Allan Nevins*[1]

And be not conformed to this world: but be ye transformed by the renewing of your mind, that ye may prove what is that good, and acceptable, and perfect, will of God.

—*Romans 12:2*

If the world hate you, ye know that it hated me before it hated you.

If ye were of the world, the world would love his own: but because ye are not of the world, but I have chosen you out of the world, therefore the world hateth you.

Remember the word that I said unto you, The servant is not greater than his lord. If they have persecuted me, they will also persecute you; if they have kept my saying, they will keep yours also.

But all these things will they do unto you for my name's sake, because they know not him that sent me.

If I had not come and spoken unto them, they had not had sin: but now they have no cloak for their sin.

He that hateth me hateth my Father also.

If I had not done among them the works which none other man did, they had not had sin: but now have they both seen and hated both me and my Father.

But this cometh to pass, that the word might be fulfilled that is written in their law, They hated me without a cause.

—*John 15:18–25*

Developing Perseverance

Resolve, and keep your resolution; choose, and pursue your choice. If you spend the day in study, you will find yourself still more able to study tomorrow; not that you are to expect that you shall at once obtain a complete victory. Depravity is not very easily overcome. Resolution will sometimes relax, and diligence will sometimes be interrupted. But let no accidental surprise or deviation, whether short or long, dispose you to despondency. Consider these failings as incident to all mankind. Begin again where you left off, and endeavor to avoid the seducements that prevailed over you before.

—Samuel Johnson

Laban said unto Jacob, Because thou art my brother, shouldest thou therefore serve me for nought? tell me, what shall thy wages be?

And Laban had two daughters: the name of the elder was Leah, and the name of the younger was Rachel.

Leah was tender eyed; but Rachel was beautiful and well-favored.

And Jacob loved Rachel; and said, I will serve thee seven years for Rachel thy younger daughter.

And Laban said, It is better that I give her to thee, than that I should give her to another man: abide with me.

And Jacob served seven years for Rachel; and they seemed unto him but a few days, for the love he had to her.

—*Genesis 29:15–20*

By much slothfulness the building decayeth; and through idleness of the hands the house droppeth through.

—*Ecclesiastes 10:18*

Although the fig tree shall not blossom, neither shall fruit be in the vines; the labor of the olive shall fail, and the fields shall yield no meat; the flock shall be cut off from the fold, and there shall be no herd in the stalls:

Yet I will rejoice in the LORD, I will joy in the God of my salvation.

The LORD God is my strength, and he will make my feet like hinds' feet, and he will make me to walk upon mine high places.

—Habbakkuk 3:17–19a

He said unto them, Which of you shall have a friend, and shall go unto him at midnight, and say unto him, Friend, lend me three loaves;

For a friend of mine in his journey is come to me, and I have nothing to set before him?

And he from within shall answer and say, Trouble me not: the door is now shut, and my children are with me in bed; I cannot rise and give thee.

I say unto you, Though he will not rise and give him, because he is his friend, yet because of his importunity he will rise and give him as many as he needeth.

And I say unto you, Ask, and it shall be given you; seek, and ye shall find; knock, and it shall be opened unto you.

For everyone that asketh receiveth; and he that seeketh findeth; and to him that knocketh it shall be opened.

—Luke 11:5–10

Be not deceived; God is not mocked: for what-soever a man soweth, that shall he also reap.

For he that soweth to his flesh shall of the flesh reap corruption; but he that soweth to the Spirit shall of the Spirit reap life everlasting.

And let us not be weary in well-doing: for in due season we shall reap, if we faint not.

—*Galatians 6:7–9*

Not as though I had already attained, either were already perfect: but I follow after, if that I may apprehend that for which also I am apprehended of Christ Jesus.

Brethren, I count not myself to have appre-hended: but this one thing I do, forgetting those things which are behind, and reaching forth unto those things which are before,

I press toward the mark for the prize of the high calling of God in Christ Jesus.

—*Philippians 3:12–14*

Growing in Faith

Through this dark and stormy night
faith beholds a feeble light
Up the blackness streaking;
Knowing God's own time is best,
In a patient hope I rest
For the full day-breaking!

—John Greenleaf Whittier

For with God nothing shall be impossible.

—*Luke 1:37*

Now faith is the substance of things hoped for, the evidence of things not seen.

For by it the elders obtained a good report.

Through faith we understand that the worlds were framed by the word of God, so that things which are seen were not made of things which do appear.

—*Hebrews 11:1–3*

For verily I say unto you, If ye have faith as a grain of mustard seed, ye shall say unto this mountain, Remove hence to yonder place;

and it shall remove; and nothing shall be
impossible unto you.

—Matthew 17:20b

For whatsoever is born of God overcometh
the world: and this is the victory that overcometh the world, even our faith. . . .

And this is the confidence that we have in
him, that, if we ask any thing according to his
will, he heareth us:

And if we know that he hear us, whatsoever
we ask, we know that we have the petitions
that we desired of him.

—1 John 5:4, 14–15

Deepening Compassion

A little girl was sent on an errand by her mother. She took much too long in coming back. Mother, therefore, demanded an explanation when she finally did return. The little girl explained that on her way she had met a little friend who was crying because she had broken her doll.

"Oh," said the mother, "then you stopped to help her fix her doll?"

"Oh, no," replied the little girl.

"I stopped to help her cry."

Like as a father pitieth his children, so the LORD pitieth them that fear him.

—*Psalm 103:13*

Therefore all things whatsoever ye would that men should do to you, do ye even so to them: for this is the law and the prophets.

—*Matthew 7:12*

This I recall to my mind, therefore have I hope. It is of the LORD'S mercies that we are not consumed, because his compassions fail not.

—*Lamentations 3:21–22*

Who is a God like unto thee, that pardoneth iniquity, and passeth by the transgression of the remnant of his heritage? he retaineth not his anger forever, because he delighteth in mercy.

He will turn again, he will have compassion upon us; he will subdue our iniquities; and thou wilt cast all their sins into the depths of the sea.

Thou wilt perform the truth to Jacob, and the mercy to Abraham, which thou hast sworn unto our fathers from the days of old.

—*Micah 7:18–20*

And Jesus went about all the cities and villages, teaching in their synagogues, and preaching the gospel of the kingdom, and healing every sickness and every disease among the people.

But when he saw the multitudes, he was moved with compassion on them, because they fainted, and were scattered abroad, as sheep having no shepherd.

—*Matthew 9:35–36*

Then shall the King say unto them on his right hand, Come, ye blessed of my Father, inherit the kingdom prepared for you from the foundation of the world:

For I was an hungered, and ye gave me meat: I was thirsty, and ye gave me drink: I was a stranger, and ye took me in:

Naked, and ye clothed me: I was sick, and ye visited me: I was in prison, and ye came unto me.

Then shall the righteous answer him, saying, Lord, when saw we thee an hungered, and fed thee? or thirsty, and gave thee drink?

When saw we thee a stranger, and took thee in? or naked, and clothed thee?

Or when saw we thee sick, or in prison, and came unto thee?

And the King shall answer and say unto them, Verily I say unto you, Inasmuch as ye have done it unto one of the least of these my brethren, ye have done it unto me.

—*Matthew 25:34–40*

And of some have compassion, making
a difference:

And others save with fear, pulling them out
of the fire; hating even the garment spotted by
the flesh.

—*Jude 22–23*

Putting on Trustworthiness

*No man is completely independent. Each of us
is responsible to others and to God. Many of
our mental ills are due to our revolt against
authority. The only way actually to be free is
to submit to controls. Aristotle said: "Freedom
is obedience to self-formulated rules." It
would be more correct to say that freedom lies
in obedience to the laws of God. Insofar as we
bend our wills to the will of God, and are
responsible to Him, we are free.*

—*Lawrence Fitzgerald*

God blessed them, and God said unto
them, Be fruitful, and multiply, and replenish
the earth, and subdue it: and have dominion

over the fish of the sea, and over the fowl of the air, and over every living thing that moveth upon the earth.

And God said, Behold, I have given you every herb bearing seed, which is upon the face of all the earth, and every tree, in the which is the fruit of a tree yielding seed; to you it shall be for meat.

And to every beast of the earth, and to every fowl of the air, and to everything that creepeth upon the earth, wherein there is life, I have given every green herb for meat: and it was so.

—*Genesis 1:28–30*

Yet they tempted and provoked the most high God, and kept not his testimonies:

But turned back, and dealt unfaithfully like their fathers: they were turned aside like a deceitful bow.

For they provoked him to anger with their high places, and moved him to jealousy with their graven images.

When God heard this, he was wroth, and greatly abhorred Israel:

So that he forsook the tabernacle of Shiloh, the tent which he placed among men;

And delivered his strength into captivity, and his glory into the enemy's hand.

He gave his people over also unto the sword; and was wroth with his inheritance.

The fire consumed their young men; and their maidens were not given to marriage.

Their priests fell by the sword; and their widows made no lamentation.

—*Psalm 78:56–64*

A talebearer revealeth secrets: but he that is of a faithful spirit concealeth the matter.

—*Proverbs 11:13*

Therefore, brethren, we are debtors, not to the flesh, to live after the flesh.

For if ye live after the flesh, ye shall die: but if ye through the Spirit do mortify the deeds of the body, ye shall live.

—*Romans 8:12–13*

They that are Christ's have crucified the flesh with the affections and lusts.

—*Galatians 5:24*

For the grace of God that bringeth salvation hath appeared to all men,

Teaching us that, denying ungodliness and worldly lusts, we should live soberly, righteously, and godly, in this present world.

—*Titus 2:11–12*

Exercising Humility

O Father, give us the humility which
Realizes its ignorance,
Admits its ignorance,
Recognizes its need,
Welcomes advice,
Accepts rebuke.
Help us always
To praise rather than to criticize,
To sympathize rather than to condemn,
To encourage rather than to discourage,
To build rather than to destroy,
And to think of people at their best
rather than at their worst.
This we ask for thy name's sake.

—*William Barclay*

In those days came John the Baptist, preaching in the wilderness of Judea,

And saying, Repent ye: for the kingdom of heaven is at hand.

For this is he that was spoken of by the prophet Isaiah, saying, The voice of one crying in the wilderness, Prepare ye the way of the Lord, make his paths straight.

And the same John had his raiment of camel's hair, and a leathern girdle about his loins; and his meat was locusts and wild honey. . . .

I indeed baptize you with water unto repentance: but he that cometh after me is mightier than I, whose shoes I am not worthy to bear: he shall baptize you with the Holy Ghost, and with fire.

Matthew 3:1–4, 11

Surely he scorneth the scorners: but he giveth grace unto the lowly.

—Proverbs 3:34

The fear of the LORD is the instruction of wisdom; and before honor is humility.

—Proverbs 15:33

Whosoever therefore shall confess me before men, him will I confess also before my Father which is in heaven.

But whosoever shall deny me before men, him will I also deny before my Father which is in heaven.

—Matthew 10:32–33

Ye adulterers and adulteresses, know ye not that the friendship of the world is enmity with God? whosoever therefore will be a friend of the world is the enemy of God. . . .

But he giveth more grace. Wherefore he saith, God resisteth the proud, but giveth grace unto the humble.

—James 4:4, 6

Humble yourselves therefore under the mighty hand of God, that he may exalt you in due time.

—1 Peter 5:6

Six

Disciplining with Love

"It seems like all I do anymore is yell at the kids," said Roberto. "Are they getting worse, or am I just getting less patient?"

How is it with you? Has the biblical call to discipline your children turned into an endless round of shouting matches? If so, what can you do to change the situation?

The Scriptures in this chapter invite us to slow down and think about our own relationship to authority and correction. After all, our children will learn more from what they see in us than from what we try to tell them.

⋘ Be Open to Correction— Yourself!

O most tender and gentle Lord Jesus,

when will my heart have a portion
of thy perfections?

When will my hard and stony heart,
my proud heart,

my unbelieving, my impure heart,
my narrow selfish heart,

be melted and conformed to thine?

O teach me . . .

to love thee sincerely and simply

as thou hast loved me.

—*John Henry Newman*

Teach me, and I will hold my tongue: and
cause me to understand wherein I have erred.

—*Job 6:24*

The fear of the LORD is the beginning of
wisdom: and the knowledge of the holy is
understanding.

—*Proverbs 9:10*

Create in me a clean heart, O God; and renew a right spirit within me....

The sacrifices of God are a broken spirit: a broken and a contrite heart, O God, thou wilt not despise.

—Psalm 51:10, 17

My son, despise not the chastening of the LORD; neither be weary of his correction:

For whom the LORD loveth he correcteth; even as a father the son in whom he delighteth.

—Proverbs 3:11–12

He, that being often reproved hardeneth his neck, shall suddenly be destroyed, and that without remedy....

A man's pride shall bring him low: but honor shall uphold the humble in spirit.

—Proverbs 29:1, 23

Exercise Accountability in Your Own Life

Sin always tends to make us blind to our own faults. We need a friend to stop us from deceiving ourselves that what we are doing is not so bad after all. We need a friend to help us overcome our low-image, inflated self-importance, selfishness, pride, our deceitful nature, our dangerous fantasies, and so much else.

—James Houston[1]

⫷ *In Your Choice of Friends*

Blessed is the man that walketh not in the counsel of the ungodly, nor standeth in the way of sinners, nor sitteth in the seat of the scornful.

But his delight is in the law of the LORD; and in his law doth he meditate day and night.

And he shall be like a tree planted by the rivers of water, that bringeth forth his fruit in his season; his leaf also shall not wither; and whatsoever he doeth shall prosper.

The ungodly are not so: but are like the chaff which the wind driveth away.

Therefore the ungodly shall not stand in the judgment, nor sinners in the congregation of the righteous.

For the LORD knoweth the way of the righteous: but the way of the ungodly shall perish.

—*Psalm 1*

Develop an Atmosphere of Family Honesty

Lie not; but let they heart be true to God.
Thy mouth to it, thy actions to them both.
Cowards tell lies, and those that fear the rod;
the stormy working soul spits lies and froth.
Dare to be true. Nothing can need a lie:
a fault which needs it most,
grows two thereby.

—*George Herbert*

The earth is the LORD'S, and the fullness thereof; the world, and they that dwell therein.

For he hath founded it upon the seas, and established it upon the floods.

Who shall ascend into the hill of the LORD? or who shall stand in his holy place?

He that hath clean hands, and a pure heart; who hath not lifted up his soul unto vanity, nor sworn deceitfully.

—*Psalm 24:1–4*

A naughty person, a wicked man, walketh with a froward mouth.

He winketh with his eyes, he speaketh with his feet, he teacheth with his fingers;

Frowardness is in his heart, he deviseth mischief continually; he soweth discord.

Therefore shall his calamity come suddenly; suddenly shall he be broken without remedy.

These six things doth the LORD hate: yea, seven are an abomination unto him:

A proud look, a lying tongue, and hands that shed innocent blood,

An heart that deviseth wicked imaginations, feet that be swift in running to mischief,

A false witness that speaketh lies, and he that soweth discord among brethren.

—*Proverbs 6:12–19*

Lie not one to another, seeing that ye have put off the old man with his deeds;

And have put on the new man, which is renewed in knowledge after the image of him that created him.

—*Colossians 3:9–10*

But above all things, my brethren, swear not, neither by heaven, neither by the earth, neither by any other oath: but let your yea be yea; and your nay, nay; lest ye fall into condemnation.

—*James 5:12*

Teach Obedience to God's Commands

Obedience must be the struggle and desire of our life. Obedience, not hard and forced, but ready, loving and spontaneous; the doing of duty, not merely that the duty may be done, but that the soul in doing it may become capable of receiving and uttering God.

—*Phillips Brooks*

Keep my commandments, and live; and my law as the apple of thine eye.

—*Proverbs 7:2*

And thou shalt love the LORD thy God with all thine heart, and with all thy soul, and with all thy might.

—*Deuteronomy 6:5*

Hereby we do know that we know him, if we keep his commandments.

—*1 John 2:3*

Whether therefore ye eat, or drink, or whatsoever ye do, do all to the glory of God.

—*1 Corinthians 10:31*

Require Respect from Your Children

Always tell your children as much of the truth as they can understand, if only to establish the most valuable attribute you have as a parent—your credibility. If you con your three-year-old into believing that the booster shot won't hurt, why should he or she believe your later claims that marijuana, booze and skipping school will?

—*Stan and Jan Berenstain*[2]

He that spareth his rod hateth his son: but he that loveth him chasteneth him betimes. . . .

Correct thy son, and he shall give thee rest; yea, he shall give delight unto thy soul.

—Proverbs 13:24; 29:17

Withhold not correction from the child: for if thou beatest him with the rod, he shall not die.

—Proverbs 23:13

Or what man is there of you, whom if his son ask bread, will he give him a stone?

Or if he ask a fish, will he give him a serpent?

If ye then, being evil, know how to give good gifts unto your children, how much more shall your Father which is in heaven give good things to them that ask him?

—Matthew 7:9–11

Teach Self-Discipline

The world is too much with us;
late and soon,
Getting and spending, we lay
waste our powers:
Little we see in Nature that is ours;
We have given our hearts away,
a sordid boon!

—William Wordsworth

Thou therefore, my son, be strong in the grace that is in Christ Jesus.

And the things that thou hast heard of me among many witnesses, the same commit thou to faithful men, who shall be able to teach others also.

Thou therefore endure hardness, as a good soldier of Jesus Christ.

—2 Timothy 2:1–3

But I say unto you, That ye resist not evil: but whosoever shall smite thee on thy right cheek, turn to him the other also.

And if any man will sue thee at the law, and take away thy coat, let him have thy cloak also.

And whosoever shall compel thee to go a mile, go with him twain.

—Matthew 5:39–41

Therefore, brethren, we are debtors, not to the flesh, to live after the flesh.

For if ye live after the flesh, ye shall die: but if ye through the Spirit do mortify the deeds of the body, ye shall live.

—Romans 8:12–13

For the grace of God that bringeth salvation hath appeared to all men,

Teaching us that, denying ungodliness and worldly lusts, we should live soberly, righteously, and godly, in this present world.

—Titus 2:11–12

Look to God for Your Parenting Skills

Doing an activity with your kids is more important than trying to devise a teaching session, says author/businessman Patrick Morley. He explains, "My son wanted to help change a flat tire on my car. He couldn't loosen the lug nuts. He ran out of energy to unscrew them all. He couldn't lift the old tire off or put the new one on. Once the new tire was on, he tried to get away with only putting on every other lug nut. It took twice as long with his help.

While he couldn't help me as much as he thought he could, he went away thinking he had helped me more than he did. The experience made a large spiritual impression on him. His self-esteem grew by a mile, and now he understands the concepts of diligence and excellence in a deeper way. Those are biblical values, and I impressed them upon my son in a way that was natural, not contrived. I wasn't teaching him how to change a flat tire; I was teaching him how to be a man of God.

—Patrick Morley[3]

A father of the fatherless, and a judge of the widows, is God in his holy habitation.

—*Psalm 68:5*

But now, O LORD, thou art our father; we are the clay, and thou our potter; and we all are the work of thy hand.

—*Isaiah 64:8*

Because ye are sons, God hath sent forth the Spirit of his Son into your hearts, crying, Abba, Father.

Wherefore thou art no more a servant, but a son; and if a son, then an heir of God through Christ.

—*Galatians 4:6–7*

⋘ *He Is a Good, Loving, and Comforting Parent*

Oh how great is thy goodness, which thou hast laid up for them that fear thee; which thou hast wrought for them that trust in thee before the sons of men!

Thou shalt hide them in the secret of thy presence from the pride of man: thou shalt keep them secretly in a pavilion from the strife of tongues.

—*Psalm 31:19–20*

For I am persuaded, that neither death, nor life, nor angels, nor principalities, nor powers, nor things present, nor things to come,

Nor height, nor depth, nor any other creature, shall be able to separate us from the love of God, which is in Christ Jesus our Lord.

—*Romans 8:38–39*

Behold, what manner of love the Father hath bestowed upon us, that we should be called the sons of God.

—*1 John 3:1a*

As one whom his mother comforteth, so will I comfort you; and ye shall be comforted.

—*Isaiah 66:13a*

For he maketh sore, and bindeth up: he woundeth, and his hands make whole.

Job 5:18

Blessed be God, even the Father of our Lord Jesus Christ, the Father of mercies, and the God of all comfort;

Who comforteth us in all our tribulation, that we may be able to comfort them which are in any trouble, by the comfort wherewith we ourselves are comforted of God.

—2 Corinthians 1:3–4

⋘ *He Accepts His Children*

But in every nation he that feareth him, and worketh righteousness, is accepted with him.

—Acts 10:35

But God, who is rich in mercy, for his great love wherewith he loved us,

Even when we were dead in sins, hath quickened us together with Christ, (by grace ye are saved;)

And hath raised us up together, and made us sit together in heavenly places in Christ Jesus:

That in the ages to come he might show the exceeding riches of his grace in his kindness toward us through Christ Jesus.

For by grace are ye saved through faith; and that not of yourselves: it is the gift of God: Not of works, lest any man should boast.

—Ephesians 2:4–9

Ye also, as lively stones, are built up a spiritual house, an holy priesthood, to offer up spiritual sacrifices, acceptable to God by Jesus Christ.

—1 Peter 2:5

⋘ *He Listens and Answers*

For thou hast heard me from the horns of the unicorns.

I will declare thy name unto my brethren: in the midst of the congregation will I praise thee.

Ye that fear the LORD, praise him; all ye the seed of Jacob, glorify him; and fear him, all ye the seed of Israel.

For he hath not despised nor abhorred the affliction of the afflicted; neither hath he hid his face from him; but when he cried unto him, he heard.

—Psalm 22:21b–24

⋘ *He Trains and Guides*

But God led the people about, through the way of the wilderness of the Red sea: and the children of Israel went up harnessed out of the land of Egypt. . . .

And the LORD went before them by day in a pillar of a cloud, to lead them the way; and by night in a pillar of fire, to give them light; to go by day and night:

He took not away the pillar of the cloud by day, nor the pillar of fire by night, from before the people.

—Exodus 13:18, 21–22

He shall feed his flock like a shepherd: he shall gather the lambs with his arm, and carry them in his bosom, and shall gently lead those that are with young.

—Isaiah 40:11

Submission Brings Joy

Is there any greater wretchedness than to taste the dregs of our own insufficiency and misery and hopelessness, and to know that we are certainly worth nothing at all? Yet it is blessed to be reduced to these depths if, in them, we can find God. Until we have reached the bottom of the abyss, there is still something for us to choose between all and nothing. There is still something in between. We can still evade the decision. When we are reduced to our last extreme, there is no further evasion. The choice is a terrible one. It is made in the heart of darkness, but with an intuition that is unbearable by its angelic clarity: when we who have been destroyed and seem to be in hell miraculously choose God!

—*Thomas Merton*

Verily, verily, I say unto you, That ye shall weep and lament, but the world shall rejoice: and ye shall be sorrowful, but your sorrow shall be turned into joy.

—*John 16:20*

For his anger endureth but a moment; in his favor is life: weeping may endure for a night, but joy cometh in the morning.

—*Psalm 30:5*

But though he cause grief, yet will he have compassion according to the multitude of his mercies.

—*Lamentations 3:32*

Seven

Keeping Your Marriage Strong

Certain things we do can destroy a marriage. We hear about those things all the time: adultery, lack of communication, money problems, pure selfishness on so many levels. But the Scriptures call us to look at the things we can do to make a marriage stronger. This is a thor-

oughly positive approach to growing in love for our spouse. And that's the way it should be, because God invented marriage and He wants it to bring us happiness for a lifetime.

Remember that God Invented Marriage

A good marriage is not a contract between two persons but a sacred covenant between three. Too often Christ is never invited to the wedding and finds no room in the home. Why? Is it because we have misrepresented Him and forgotten His joyful outlook on life?

—*Donald T. Kauffman*[1]

The LORD God said, It is not good that the man should be alone; I will make him an help meet for him.

And out of the ground the LORD God formed every beast of the field, and every fowl of the air; and brought them unto Adam to see what he would call them: and whatsoever

Adam called every living creature, that was the name thereof.

And Adam gave names to all cattle, and to the fowl of the air, and to every beast of the field; but for Adam there was not found an help meet for him.

And the LORD God caused a deep sleep to fall upon Adam, and he slept: and he took one of his ribs, and closed up the flesh instead thereof;

And the rib, which the LORD God had taken from man, made he a woman, and brought her unto the man.

And Adam said, This is now bone of my bones, and flesh of my flesh: she shall be called Woman, because she was taken out of Man.

Therefore shall a man leave his father and his mother, and shall cleave unto his wife: and they shall be one flesh.

—Genesis 2:18–24

Do Things that Strengthen a Marriage

Marriage is a school where we learn to be flexible, to live in harmony with each other, to walk together as one, to strengthen and complement each other as we fulfill our corporate and individual dreams, hopes, and ambitions in our journey through life.

—H. Norman Wright[2]

When a man hath taken a new wife, he shall not go out to war, neither shall he be charged with any business: but he shall be free at home one year, and shall cheer up his wife which he hath taken.

—Deuteronomy 24:5

⋘ Say to Your Spouse: "You're Beautiful to Me!"

Then she fell on her face, and bowed herself to the ground, and said unto him, Why have I found grace in thine eyes, that thou shouldest take knowledge of me, seeing I am a stranger?

—*Ruth 2:10*

Behold, thou art fair, my love; behold, thou art fair; thou hast doves' eyes within thy locks: thy hair is as a flock of goats, that appear from mount Gilead.

Thy teeth are like a flock of sheep that are even shorn, which came up from the washing; whereof everyone bear twins, and none is barren among them.

Thy lips are like a thread of scarlet, and thy speech is comely: thy temples are like a piece of a pomegranate within thy locks.

Thy neck is like the tower of David builded for an armory, whereon there hang a thousand bucklers, all shields of mighty men.

Thy two breasts are like two young roes that are twins, which feed among the lilies.

Until the day break, and the shadows flee away, I will get me to the mountain of myrrh, and to the hill of frankincense.

Thou art all fair, my love; there is no spot in thee.

—*Song of Solomon 4:1–7*

Drink waters out of thine own cistern, and running waters out of thine own well.

Let thy fountains be dispersed abroad, and rivers of waters in the streets.

Let them be only thine own, and not strangers' with thee.

Let thy fountain be blessed: and rejoice with the wife of thy youth.

Let her be as the loving hind and pleasant roe; let her breasts satisfy thee at all times; and be thou ravished always with her love.

And why wilt thou, my son, be ravished with a strange woman, and embrace the bosom of a stranger?

—Proverbs 5:15–20

⋘ *Honor God Together*

Know therefore that the LORD thy God, he is God, the faithful God, which keepeth covenant and mercy with them that love him and keep his commandments to a thousand generations.

—Deuteronomy 7:9

Delight thyself also in the LORD; and he shall give thee the desires of thine heart.

—*Psalm 37:4*

I love them that love me; and those that seek me early shall find me.

—*Proverbs 8:17*

He that hath my commandments, and keepeth them, he it is that loveth me: and he that loveth me shall be loved of my Father, and I will love him, and will manifest myself to him.

—*John 14:21*

⋘ *Keep the Communication Lines Open*

A soft answer turneth away wrath: but grievous words stir up anger.

—*Proverbs 15:1*

A scorner loveth not one that reproveth him: neither will he go unto the wise.

—*Proverbs 15:12*

A brother offended is harder to be won than a strong city: and their contentions are like the bars of a castle.

—*Proverbs 18:19*

A foolish son is the calamity of his father: and the contentions of a wife are a continual dropping.

—*Proverbs 19:13*

Blessed are ye, when men shall revile you, and persecute you, and shall say all manner of evil against you falsely, for my sake.

Rejoice, and be exceeding glad: for great is your reward in heaven: for so persecuted they the prophets which were before you.

—*Matthew 5:11–12*

With all lowliness and meekness, with longsuffering, forbearing one another in love;

Endeavoring to keep the unity of the Spirit in the bond of peace.

—*Ephesians 4:2–3*

But speaking the truth in love, may grow up into him in all things, which is the head, even Christ:

From whom the whole body fitly joined together and compacted by that which every joint supplieth, according to the effectual working in the measure of every part, maketh increase of the body unto the edifying of itself in love.

—*Ephesians 4:15–16*

Speaking to yourselves in psalms and hymns and spiritual songs, singing and making melody in your heart to the Lord;

Giving thanks always for all things unto God and the Father in the name of our Lord Jesus Christ.

—*Ephesians 5:19–20*

Forbearing one another, and forgiving one another, if any man have a quarrel against any: even as Christ forgave you, so also do ye.

And above all these things put on charity, which is the bond of perfectness.

—*Colossians 3:13–14*

Having a good conscience; that, whereas they speak evil of you, as of evildoers, they may be ashamed that falsely accuse your good conversation in Christ.

For it is better, if the will of God be so, that ye suffer for welldoing, than for evildoing.

—1 Peter 3:16–17

⋘ Avoid Sexual Temptation

Watch and pray, that ye enter not into temptation: the spirit indeed is willing, but the flesh is weak.

—Matthew 26:41

I made a covenant with mine eyes; why then should I think upon a maid? . . .

If mine heart have been deceived by a woman, or if I have laid wait at my neighbor's door;

Then let my wife grind unto another, and let others bow down upon her.

For this is an heinous crime; yea, it is an iniquity to be punished by the judges.

For it is a fire that consumeth to destruction, and would root out all mine increase.

—Job 31:1, 9–12

For this is the will of God, even your sanctification, that ye should abstain from fornication:

That every one of you should know how to possess his vessel in sanctification and honor;

Not in the lust of concupiscence, even as the Gentiles which know not God:

That no man go beyond and defraud his brother in any matter: because that the Lord is the avenger of all such, as we also have forewarned you and testified.

For God hath not called us unto uncleanness, but unto holiness.

He therefore that despiseth, despiseth not man, but God, who hath also given unto us his holy Spirit.

—*1 Thessalonians 4:3–8*

My brethren, count it all joy when ye fall into divers temptations;

Knowing this, that the trying of your faith worketh patience.

But let patience have her perfect work, that ye may be perfect and entire, wanting nothing. . . .

Blessed is the man that endureth temptation: for when he is tried, he shall receive the crown of life, which the Lord hath promised to them that love him.

—*James 1:2–4, 12*

Follow the Example of a Good Marriage

Marriage is like a three-speed gearbox: affection, friendship, love. It is not advisable to crash you gears and go right through to love straightaway. You need to ease your way through. The basis of love is respect, and that needs to be learned from affection and friendship.

—*Peter Ustinov*[3]

Then said Boaz unto his servant that was set over the reapers, Whose damsel is this?

And the servant that was set over the reapers answered and said, It is the Moabitish damsel that came back with Naomi out of the country of Moab:

And she said, I pray you, let me glean and gather after the reapers among the sheaves: so she came, and hath continued even from the morning until now, that she tarried a little in the house.

Then said Boaz unto Ruth, Hearest thou not, my daughter? Go not to glean in another field, neither go from hence, but abide here fast by my maidens:

Let thine eyes be on the field that they do reap, and go thou after them: have I not charged the young men that they shall not touch thee? and when thou art athirst, go unto the vessels, and drink of that which the young men have drawn.

Then she fell on her face, and bowed herself to the ground, and said unto him, Why have I found grace in thine eyes, that thou shouldest take knowledge of me, seeing I am a stranger?

—*Ruth 2:5–10*

So Boaz took Ruth, and she was his wife: and when he went in unto her, the LORD gave her conception, and she bare a son.

And the women said unto Naomi, Blessed be the LORD, which hath not left thee this day without a kinsman, that his name may be famous in Israel.

And he shall be unto thee a restorer of thy life, and a nourisher of thine old age: for thy daughter-in-law, which loveth thee, which is better to thee than seven sons, hath born him.

—Ruth 4:13–15

Recognize the Spiritual Significance of Marriage

When we yearn for life-giving relationships with any person or part of creation, we are at the very same time reaching for God. For, according to an incarnationalist faith, God is the spiritual presence who becomes incarnate in and through creaturely flesh. Another way of saying this is that we are simply longing for more life-giving connectedness between our sexuality and our spirituality.

—James B. Nelson[4]

For thy Maker is thine husband; the LORD of hosts is his name; and thy Redeemer the

Holy One of Israel; The God of the whole
earth shall he be called.

—*Isaiah 54:5*

Turn, O backsliding children, saith the
LORD; for I am married unto you: and I will
take you one of a city, and two of a family, and
I will bring you to Zion.

—*Jeremiah 3:14*

Not according to the covenant that I made
with their fathers in the day that I took them
by the hand to bring them out of the land of
Egypt; which my covenant they brake,
although I was an husband unto them, saith
the LORD.

—*Jeremiah 31:32*

Be ye therefore followers of God, as dear
children; . . .

Submitting yourselves one to another in
the fear of God.

Wives, submit yourselves unto your own
husbands, as unto the Lord.

For the husband is the head of the wife,
even as Christ is the head of the church: and
he is the savior of the body.

Therefore as the church is subject unto Christ, so let the wives be to their own husbands in everything.

Husbands, love your wives, even as Christ also loved the church, and gave himself for it;

That he might sanctify and cleanse it with the washing of water by the word,

That he might present it to himself a glorious church, not having spot, or wrinkle, or any such thing; but that it should be holy and without blemish.

So ought men to love their wives as their own bodies. He that loveth his wife loveth himself.

For no man ever yet hated his own flesh; but nourisheth and cherisheth it, even as the Lord the church:

For we are members of his body, of his flesh, and of his bones.

For this cause shall a man leave his father and mother, and shall be joined unto his wife, and they two shall be one flesh.

This is a great mystery: but I speak concerning Christ and the church.

—*Ephesians 5:1, 21–32*

Staying Healthy

*K*eeping ourselves healthy is important—not just to us, but to our entire family. Our spouses depend on us, and so do our children. Even though good health is a gift (if we have it), no matter what the state of our health, we're responsible to pursue the things that nurture our minds and bodies. God gives us some wonderful promises in the Word to encourage us along the way.

Maintaining Physical Health

Look to your health; and if you have it, praise
God, and value it next to a good conscience.
For health is the second blessing that we
mortals are capable of—
a blessing that money cannot buy.

—*Izaak Walton*

Beloved, I wish above all things that thou
mayest prosper and be in health, even as thy
soul prospereth.

—*3 John 2*

⋘ *Making Time for Yourself*

Walk in wisdom toward them that are
without, redeeming the time.

—*Colossians 4:5*

But this I say, brethren, the time is short.
—*1 Corinthians 7:29a*

Whereas ye know not what shall be on the morrow. For what is your life? It is even a vapor, that appeareth for a little time, and then vanisheth away.

—James 4:14

⋘ *Making Time for Exercise*

When thou goest, thy steps shall not be straitened; and when thou runnest, thou shalt not stumble.

—Proverbs 4:12

For by thee I have run through a troop: by my God have I leaped over a wall.

—2 Samuel 22:30

I beseech you therefore, brethren, by the mercies of God, that ye present your bodies a living sacrifice, holy, acceptable unto God, which is your reasonable service.

—Romans 12:1

What? know ye not that your body is the temple of the Holy Ghost which is in you, which ye have of God, and ye are not your own?

For ye are bought with a price: therefore glorify God in your body, and in your spirit, which are God's.

—*1 Corinthians 6:19–20*

≪ *Watching Your Nutrition*

There is nothing better for a man, than that he should eat and drink, and that he should make his soul enjoy good in his labor. This also I saw, that it was from the hand of God.

—*Ecclesiastes 2:24*

In the multitude of my thoughts within me thy comforts delight my soul.

—*Psalm 94:19*

For none of us liveth to himself, and no man dieth to himself.

For whether we live, we live unto the Lord; and whether we die, we die unto the Lord: whether we live therefore, or die, we are the Lord's.

—*Romans 14:7–8*

⋘ *Getting Enough Sleep*

I laid me down and slept; I awaked; for the LORD sustained me.

—*Psalm 3:5*

And when he was entered into a ship, his disciples followed him.

And, behold, there arose a great tempest in the sea, insomuch that the ship was covered with the waves: but he was asleep.

—*Matthew 8:23–24*

Pursuing Emotional Health

The people I know who truly like themselves as persons, apart from their roles in life as husband, wife, parent, or job-holder, are those who have learned to be honest with themselves and who to some degree understand themselves.... Honesty with oneself, with God, and with one's fellow man is the first all important step in spiritual and emotional growth.

—*Cecil Osborne*[1]

⋘ *Honestly Facing What's Inside . . .*

For I know that in me (that is, in my flesh,) dwelleth no good thing: for to will is present with me; but how to perform that which is good I find not.

For the good that I would I do not: but the evil which I would not, that I do.

Now if I do that I would not, it is no more I that do it, but sin that dwelleth in me.

—*Romans 7:18–20*

For we dare not make ourselves of the number, or compare ourselves with some that commend themselves; but they measuring themselves by themselves, and comparing themselves among themselves, are not wise. . . .

Examine yourselves, whether ye be in the faith; prove your own selves. Know ye not your own selves, how that Jesus Christ is in you, except ye be reprobates?

2 Corinthians 10:12; 13:5

⋘ *Confessing Secret Sins*

Who can understand his errors? cleanse thou me from secret faults.

Keep back thy servant also from presumptuous sins; let them not have dominion over me: then shall I be upright, and I shall be innocent from the great transgression.

Let the words of my mouth, and the meditation of my heart, be acceptable in thy sight, O LORD, my strength, and my redeemer.

—*Psalm 19:12–14*

If thy right eye offend thee, pluck it out, and cast it from thee: for it is profitable for thee that one of thy members should perish, and not that thy whole body should be cast into hell.

And if thy right hand offend thee, cut it off, and cast it from thee: for it is profitable for thee that one of thy members should perish, and not that thy whole body should be cast into hell.

—*Matthew 5:29–30*

⋘ *Acknowledging Inner Pain*

For mine iniquities are gone over mine head: as an heavy burden they are too heavy for me.

My wounds stink and are corrupt because of my foolishness.

I am troubled; I am bowed down greatly; I go mourning all the day long.

For my loins are filled with a loathsome disease: and there is no soundness in my flesh.

I am feeble and sore broken: I have roared by reason of the disquietness of my heart.

—*Psalm 38:4–8*

Learning to Deal with Your Feelings

For some strange reason ... man, although proud of the thinking that has led to systems of philosophy and to scientific invention, proud also of the achievements of the human will, is ashamed of his emotions.

—Leslie D. Weatherhead

⋘ *When Anger Wells Up ...*

God saw their works, that they turned from their evil way; and God repented of the evil, that he had said that he would do unto them; and he did it not.

—Jonah 3:10

Stand in awe, and sin not: commune with your own heart upon your bed, and be still.

—Psalm 4:4

But I say unto you, That whosoever is angry with his brother without a cause shall be in danger of the judgment: and whosoever shall say to his brother, Raca, shall be in danger of the council: but whosoever shall say, Thou fool, shall be in danger of hell fire.

—Matthew 5:22

Be ye angry, and sin not: let not the sun go down upon your wrath.

—Ephesians 4:26

⋘ *When Depression Hits...*

My soul longeth, yea, even fainteth for the courts of the LORD: my heart and my flesh crieth out for the living God.

—Psalm 84:2

When I would comfort myself against sorrow, my heart is faint in me.

—Jeremiah 8:18

When my soul fainted within me I remembered the LORD: and my prayer came in unto thee, into thine holy temple.

—Jonah 2:7

O God, thou art terrible out of thy holy places: the God of Israel is he that giveth strength and power unto his people. Blessed be God.

—*Psalm 68:35*

Come unto me, all ye that labor and are heavy laden, and I will give you rest.

Take my yoke upon you, and learn of me; for I am meek and lowly in heart: and ye shall find rest unto your souls.

For my yoke is easy, and my burden is light.

—*Matthew 11:28–30*

For though he was crucified through weakness, yet he liveth by the power of God. For we also are weak in him, but we shall live with him by the power of God toward you.

—*2 Corinthians 13:4*

Finally, my brethren, be strong in the Lord, and in the power of his might.

—*Ephsians 6:10*

⋘ *When Fear Overwhelms . . .*

Fear came upon me, and trembling, which made all my bones to shake.

—Job 4:14

My heart panted, fearfulness affrighted me: the night of my pleasure hath he turned into fear unto me.

—Isaiah 21:4

For I have heard the slander of many: fear was on every side: while they took counsel together against me, they devised to take away my life.

—Psalm 31:13

Though an host should encamp against me, my heart shall not fear: though war should rise against me, in this will I be confident.

—Psalm 27:3

For God hath not given us the spirit of fear; but of power, and of love, and of a sound mind.

2 Timothy 1:7

But whoso hearkeneth unto me shall dwell safely, and shall be quiet from fear of evil.

—*Proverbs 1:33*

Be strong and of a good courage, fear not, nor be afraid of them: for the LORD thy God, he it is that doth go with thee; he will not fail thee, nor forsake thee.

—*Deuteronomy 31:6*

Therefore will not we fear, though the earth be removed, and though the mountains be carried into the midst of the sea.

Psalm 46:2

Fear not, little flock; for it is your Father's good pleasure to give you the kingdom.

—*Luke 12:32*

There is no fear in love; but perfect love casteth out fear: because fear hath torment. He that feareth is not made perfect in love.

—*1 John 4:18*

Have not I commanded thee? Be strong and of a good courage; be not afraid, neither be thou dismayed: for the LORD thy God is with thee whithersoever thou goest.

Joshua 1:9

⋘ *When Bitterness Consumes . . .*

My soul is weary of my life; I will leave my complaint upon myself; I will speak in the bitterness of my soul.

—Job 10:1

For thy heart is not right in the sight of God.

Repent therefore of this thy wickedness, and pray God, if perhaps the thought of thine heart may be forgiven thee.

For I perceive that thou art in the gall of bitterness, and in the bond of iniquity.

—Acts 8:21b–23

Behold, for peace I had great bitterness: but thou hast in love to my soul delivered it from the pit of corruption: for thou hast cast all my sins behind thy back.

—Isaiah 38:17

Let all bitterness, and wrath, and anger, and clamor, and evil speaking, be put away from you, with all malice.

—*Ephesians 4:31*

Looking diligently lest any man fail of the grace of God; lest any root of bitterness springing up trouble you, and thereby many be defiled.

—*Hebrews 12:15*

Seeing Yourself as Loved by God

*I learned that love was our Lord's meaning.
And I saw for certain, both here and elsewhere,
that before ever he made us, God loved us;
and that his love has never slackened,
nor ever shall.
In this love all his works have been done,
and in this love he has made everything serve us;
and in this love our life is everlasting.
Our beginning was when we were made,
but the love in which he made us
never had beginning.*

In it we have our beginning.
All this we shall see in God for ever.
May Jesus grant this.

—Julian of Norwich

⋘ Created in the Image of God

So God created man in his own image, in the image of God created he him; male and female created he them.

And God blessed them, and God said unto them, Be fruitful, and multiply, and replenish the earth, and subdue it: and have dominion over the fish of the sea, and over the fowl of the air, and over every living thing that moveth upon the earth.

—Genesis 1:27–28

I will praise thee; for I am fearfully and wonderfully made: marvelous are thy works; and that my soul knoweth right well.

—Psalm 139:14

⫷ *Given a Purpose to Fulfill*

For we are his workmanship, created in Christ Jesus unto good works, which God hath before ordained that we should walk in them.

—Ephesians 2:10

Therefore if any man be in Christ, he is a new creature: old things are passed away; behold, all things are become new.

And all things are of God, who hath reconciled us to himself by Jesus Christ, and hath given to us the ministry of reconciliation;

To wit, that God was in Christ, reconciling the world unto himself, not imputing their trespasses unto them; and hath committed unto us the word of reconciliation.

Now then we are ambassadors for Christ, as though God did beseech you by us: we pray you in Christ's stead, be ye reconciled to God.

—2 Corinthians 5:17–20

That ye might walk worthy of the Lord unto all pleasing, being fruitful in every good

work, and increasing in the knowledge
of God;

Strengthened with all might, according to
his glorious power, unto all patience and
longsuffering with joyfulness;

Giving thanks unto the Father, which hath
made us meet to be partakers of the inheritance of the saints in light.

—Colossians 1:10–12

Go ye therefore, and teach all nations, bap-
tizing them in the name of the Father, and of
the Son, and of the Holy Ghost:

Teaching them to observe all things whatsoever I have commanded you: and, lo, I am
with you always, even unto the end of the
world. Amen.

—Matthew 28:19–20

Nine

Handling Work and Finances Wisely

❦

The drive for career success: it's a part of all of us. Since our job and our pay take up so much of our time and energy, we must think clearly about how they relate to our spiritual growth. We'll have to learn to adjust when our career priorities get out of sync with the principles in the Word.

We'll have to learn to pull back when workaholism threatens. (Or maybe we'll have to get up off the couch when legitimate work beckons and we're feeling downright lazy!)

Whatever the case with you, remember that the Bible offers plenty of guidance regarding work and money. Consider these promises, for example:

Feeling Worried about Money?

Riches are the pettiest and least worthy gifts which God can give a man. What are they to God's Word, to bodily gifts, such as beauty and health; or to the gifts of the mind, such as understanding, skill, wisdom?

Yet men toil for them day and night, and take not rest. Therefore God commonly gives riches to foolish people to whom he gives nothing else.

—Martin Luther

My bowels boiled, and rested not: the days of affliction prevented me.

—*Job 30:27*

I am feeble and sore broken: I have roared by reason of the disquietness of my heart.

—*Psalm 38:8*

Therefore I say unto you, Take no thought for your life, what ye shall eat, or what ye shall drink; nor yet for your body, what ye shall put on. Is not the life more than meat, and the body than raiment?

Behold the fowls of the air: for they sow not, neither do they reap, nor gather into barns; yet your heavenly Father feedeth them. Are ye not much better than they?

—*Matthew 6:25–26*

Be careful for nothing; but in everything by prayer and supplication with thanksgiving let your requests be made known unto God.

And the peace of God, which passeth all understanding, shall keep your hearts and minds through Christ Jesus. . . .

Not that I speak in respect of want: for I have learned, in whatsoever state I am, therewith to be content.

I know both how to be abased, and I know how to abound: everywhere and in all things

I am instructed both to be full and to be hungry, both to abound and to suffer need.

I can do all things through Christ which strengtheneth me.

—Philippians 4:6–7, 11–13

⫷ *Get Your Priorities Right*

Honor the LORD with thy substance, and with the firstfruits of all thine increase:

So shall thy barns be filled with plenty, and thy presses shall burst out with new wine.

—Proverbs 3:9–10

The LORD maketh poor, and maketh rich: he bringeth low, and lifteth up.

He raiseth up the poor out of the dust, and lifteth up the beggar from the dunghill, to set them among princes, and to make them inherit the throne of glory: for the pillars of the earth are the LORD'S, and he hath set the world upon them.

He will keep the feet of his saints, and the wicked shall be silent in darkness; for by strength shall no man prevail.

—1 Samuel 2:7–9

Lay not up for yourselves treasures upon earth, where moth and rust doth corrupt, and where thieves break through and steal:

But lay up for yourselves treasures in heaven, where neither moth nor rust doth corrupt, and where thieves do not break through nor steal:

For where your treasure is, there will your heart be also.

—*Matthew 6:19–21*

Let your conversation be without covetousness; and be content with such things as ye have: for he hath said, I will never leave thee, nor forsake thee.

So that we may boldly say, The Lord is my helper, and I will not fear what man shall do unto me.

Remember them which have the rule over you, who have spoken unto you the word of God: whose faith follow, considering the end of their conversation.

—*Hebrews 13:5–7*

⫷ *Use Possessions Wisely and Frugally*

He that loveth pleasure shall be a poor man: he that loveth wine and oil shall not be rich.

The wicked shall be a ransom for the righteous, and the transgressor for the upright.

It is better to dwell in the wilderness, than with a contentious and an angry woman.

There is treasure to be desired and oil in the dwelling of the wise; but a foolish man spendeth it up.

He that followeth after righteousness and mercy findeth life, righteousness, and honor.

—Proverbs 21:17–21

A good man leaveth an inheritance to his children's children: and the wealth of the sinner is laid up for the just.

—Proverbs 13:22

Be not among winebibbers; among riotous eaters of flesh:

For the drunkard and the glutton shall come to poverty: and drowsiness shall clothe a man with rags.

—Proverbs 23:20–21

They did all eat, and were filled: and they took up of the broken meat that was left seven baskets full.

—Matthew 15:37

Feeling Oppressed at Work?

No words can express how much the world owes to sorrow.

Most of the psalms were born in a wilderness.

Most of the epistles were written in a prison.

The greatest thoughts of the greatest thinkers have all passed through the fire. . . .

Take comfort, afflicted Christian!

When God is about to make preeminent use of a man,

He puts him in the fire.

—George MacDonald

Thou shalt not rule over him with rigor; but shalt fear thy God.

—Leviticus 25:43

He that oppresseth the poor to increase his riches, and he that giveth to the rich, shall surely come to want.

—*Proverbs 22:16*

And I will come near to you to judgment; and I will be a swift witness against the sorcerers, and against the adulterers, and against false swearers, and against those that oppress the hireling in his wages, the widow, and the fatherless, and that turn aside the stranger from his right, and fear not me, saith the LORD of hosts.

—*Malachi 3:5*

And he went and joined himself to a citizen of that country; and he sent him into his fields to feed swine.

And he would fain have filled his belly with the husks that the swine did eat: and no man gave unto him.

—*Luke 15:15–16*

Behold, the hire of the laborers who have reaped down your fields, which is of you kept back by fraud, crieth: and the cries of them which have reaped are entered into the ears of the Lord of Sabaoth.

—*James 5:4*

For the laborer is worthy of his hire.

—*Luke 10:7b*

⋘ *Welcome Hard Work*

He that tilleth his land shall be satisfied with bread: but he that followeth vain persons is void of understanding. . . .

The hand of the diligent shall bear rule: but the slothful shall be under tribute.

Heaviness in the heart of man maketh it stoop: but a good word maketh it glad.

The righteous is more excellent than his neighbor: but the way of the wicked seduceth them.

The slothful man roasteth not that which he took in hunting: but the substance of a diligent man is precious.

—*Proverbs 12:11, 24–27*

The ants are a people not strong, yet they prepare their meat in the summer;

The conies are but a feeble folk, yet make
they their houses in the rocks;

The locusts have no king, yet go they forth
all of them by bands;

The spider taketh hold with her hands, and
is in kings' palaces.

—*Proverbs 30:25–28*

[Be] not slothful in business; fervent in
spirit; serving the Lord.

—*Romans 12:11*

Let him that stole steal no more: but rather
let him labor, working with his hands the
thing which is good, that he may have to give
to him that needeth.

—*Ephesians 4:28*

And that ye study to be quiet, and to do
your own business, and to work with your
own hands, as we commanded you;

That ye may walk honestly toward them that
are without, and that ye may have lack of nothing.

—*1 Thessalonians 4:11–12*

For even when we were with you, this we commanded you, that if any would not work, neither should he eat.

For we hear that there are some which walk among you disorderly, working not at all, but are busybodies.

Now them that are such we command and exhort by our Lord Jesus Christ, that with quietness they work, and eat their own bread.

2 Thessalonians 3:10–12

⋘ *Avoid Untrustworthy Actions*

[Jesus] said also unto his disciples, There was a certain rich man, which had a steward; and the same was accused unto him that he had wasted his goods.

And he called him, and said unto him, How is it that I hear this of thee? give an account of thy stewardship; for thou mayest be no longer steward.

Then the steward said within himself, What shall I do? for my lord taketh away from me the stewardship: I cannot dig; to beg I am ashamed.

I am resolved what to do, that, when I am put out of the stewardship, they may receive me into their houses.

So he called everyone of his lord's debtors unto him, and said unto the first, How much owest thou unto my lord?

And he said, An hundred measures of oil. And he said unto him, Take thy bill, and sit down quickly, and write fifty.

Then said he to another, And how much owest thou? And he said, An hundred measures of wheat. And he said unto him, Take thy bill, and write fourscore.

And the lord commended the unjust steward, because he had done wisely: for the children of this world are in their generation wiser than the children of light.

And I say unto you, Make to yourselves friends of the mammon of unrighteousness; that, when ye fail, they may receive you into everlasting habitations.

He that is faithful in that which is least is faithful also in much: and he that is unjust in the least is unjust also in much.

If therefore ye have not been faithful in the unrighteous mammon, who will commit to your trust the true riches?

And if ye have not been faithful in that which is another man's, who shall give you that which is your own?

No servant can serve two masters: for either he will hate the one, and love the other; or else he will hold to the one, and despise the other. Ye cannot serve God and mammon.

—*Luke 16:1–13*

Hear another parable: There was a certain householder, which planted a vineyard, and hedged it round about, and digged a winepress in it, and built a tower, and let it out to husbandmen, and went into a far country:

And when the time of the fruit drew near, he sent his servants to the husbandmen, that they might receive the fruits of it.

And the husbandmen took his servants, and beat one, and killed another, and stoned another.

Again, he sent other servants more than the first: and they did unto them likewise.

But last of all he sent unto them his son, saying, They will reverence my son.

But when the husbandmen saw the son, they said among themselves, This is the heir; come, let us kill him, and let us seize on his inheritance.

And they caught him, and cast him out of the vineyard, and slew him.

When the lord therefore of the vineyard cometh, what will he do unto those husbandmen?

They say unto him, He will miserably destroy those wicked men, and will let out his vineyard unto other husbandmen, which shall render him the fruits in their seasons.

—Matthew 21:33–41

But he that is an hireling, and not the shepherd, whose own the sheep are not, seeth the wolf coming, and leaveth the sheep, and fleeth: and the wolf catcheth them, and scattereth the sheep.

The hireling fleeth, because he is an hireling, and careth not for the sheep.

—John 10:12–13

⋘ Know Who Your True "Employer" Is

Ye call me Master and Lord: and ye say well; for so I am.

—*John 13:13*

Know ye not, that to whom ye yield yourselves servants to obey, his servants ye are to whom ye obey; whether of sin unto death, or of obedience unto righteousness?

But God be thanked, that ye were the servants of sin, but ye have obeyed from the heart that form of doctrine which was delivered you.

Being then made free from sin, ye became the servants of righteousness.

I speak after the manner of men because of the infirmity of your flesh: for as ye have yielded your members servants to uncleanness and to iniquity unto iniquity; even so now yield your members servants to righteousness unto holiness.

For when ye were the servants of sin, ye were free from righteousness.

What fruit had ye then in those things whereof ye are now ashamed? for the end of those things is death.

But now being made free from sin, and become servants to God, ye have your fruit unto holiness, and the end everlasting life.

—*Romans 6:16–22*

Art thou called being a servant? care not for it: but if thou mayest be made free, use it rather.

For he that is called in the Lord, being a servant, is the Lord's freeman: likewise also he that is called, being free, is Christ's servant.

Ye are bought with a price; be not ye the servants of men.

—*1 Corinthians 7:21–23*

Rest in God's Peace

The Lord is my pace-setter, I shall not rush.
He makes me stop and rest for quiet intervals,
He provides me with images of stillness,
which restore my serenity.
He leads me in the ways of efficiency;
through the calmness of mind,
and his guidance is peace.
Even though I have a great many things
to accomplish each day,
I will not fret for his presence is here.
His timelessness, his all-importance,
will keep me in balance.
He prepares refreshment and renewal
in the midst of my activity.
By anointing my mind with his oils of
tranquillity,
my cup of joyous energy overflows.
Surely harmony and effectiveness
shall be the fruits of my hours,
for I shall walk in the pace of my Lord,
and dwell in his house for ever.

—*Toki Miyashina (based on Psalm 23)*[1]

Six days thou shalt do thy work, and on the seventh-day thou shalt rest: that thine ox and thine ass may rest, and the son of thy hand-maid, and the stranger, may be refreshed.

—Exodus 23:12

Thou wilt keep him in perfect peace, whose mind is stayed on thee: because he trusteth in thee.

—Isaiah 26:3

For he shall be as a tree planted by the waters, and that spreadeth out her roots by the river, and shall not see when heat cometh, but her leaf shall be green; and shall not be careful in the year of drought, neither shall cease from yielding fruit.

—Jeremiah 17:8

For God is not the author of confusion, but of peace, as in all churches of the saints.

—1 Corinthians 14:3

And the peace of God, which passeth all understanding, shall keep your hearts and minds through Christ Jesus.

—Philippians 4:7

Now the Lord of peace himself give you peace always by all means. The Lord be with you all.

—2 Thessalonians 3:16

These things I have spoken unto you, that in me ye might have peace. In the world ye shall have tribulation: but be of good cheer; I have overcome the world.

—John 16:33

Following Your Biblical Mentors

Who were your heroes when you were a kid? Who are your heroes now? Some people would say it's tougher than ever to find good role models today, but heroes are still out there. Most men can point to a man in their past—a teacher, a coach, or a neighbor—who took a special interest in them, providing guidance and wise advice at just the right time.

The Bible, of course is a great place to find mentors in spiritual growth. Here are just a few of the *standouts. All are worthy of emulation by any man seeking to put on the character of his Lord.*

Follow Your Biblical Role Models

Example is not the main thing in influencing others. It is the only thing.
—*Albert Schweitzer*

I write not these things to shame you, but as my beloved sons I warn you.

For though ye have ten thousand instructors in Christ, yet have ye not many fathers: for in Christ Jesus I have begotten you through the gospel.

Wherefore I beseech you, be ye followers of me.

—*1 Corinthians 4:14–16*

Take, my brethren, the prophets, who have spoken in the name of the Lord, for an example of suffering affliction, and of patience.

—*James 5:10*

Beloved, follow not that which is evil, but that which is good.

—*3 John 11a*

Abraham: Willingness to Risk for God

It is not the critic who counts;
not the man who points out how
the strong man stumbles,
or where the doer of deeds
could have done them better.
The credit belongs to the man
who is actually in the arena,
whose face is marred by
dust and sweat and blood;
who strives valiantly;
who errs, and comes short again and again,
because there is not effort
without error and shortcoming;
but who does actually strive to do the deeds;
who knows the great enthusiasms,
the great devotions;
who spends himself in a worthy cause;
who at best knows in the end
the triumphs of high achievement
and who at the worst, if he fails,
at least fails while daring greatly,

knowing his place shall never be
with those cold and timid souls
who know neither victory nor defeat.

—*Theodore Roosevelt*

Now the LORD had said unto Abram, Get thee out of thy country, and from thy kindred, and from thy father's house, unto a land that I will show thee:

And I will make of thee a great nation, and I will bless thee, and make thy name great; and thou shalt be a blessing:

And I will bless them that bless thee, and curse him that curseth thee: and in thee shall all families of the earth be blessed.

So Abram departed, as the LORD had spoken unto him; and Lot went with him: and Abram was seventy and five years old when he departed out of Haran.

And Abram took Sarai his wife, and Lot his brother's son, and all their substance that they had gathered, and the souls that they had gotten in Haran; and they went forth to go into the land of Canaan; and into the land of Canaan they came.

And Abram passed through the land unto the place of Sichem, unto the plain of Moreh. And the Canaanite was then in the land.

And the LORD appeared unto Abram, and said, Unto thy seed will I give this land: and there builded he an altar unto the LORD, who appeared unto him.

And he removed from thence unto a mountain on the east of Beth-el, and pitched his tent, having Beth-el on the west, and Hai on the east: and there he builded an altar unto the LORD, and called upon the name of the LORD.

And Abram journeyed, going on still toward the south.

—Genesis 12:1–9

Noah: Committing to Obedience

It is vain thought to flee from the work that God appoints us, for the sake of finding a greater blessing, instead of seeking it where alone it is to be found—in loving obedience.

—George Eliot

God looked upon the earth, and, behold, it was corrupt; for all flesh had corrupted his way upon the earth.

And God said unto Noah, The end of all flesh is come before me; for the earth is filled with violence through them; and, behold, I will destroy them with the earth.

Make thee an ark of gopher wood; rooms shalt thou make in the ark, and shalt pitch it within and without with pitch.

And this is the fashion which thou shalt make it of: The length of the ark shall be three hundred cubits, the breadth of it fifty cubits, and the height of it thirty cubits.

A window shalt thou make to the ark, and in a cubit shalt thou finish it above; and the door of the ark shalt thou set in the side thereof; with lower, second, and third stories shalt thou make it.

And, behold, I, even I, do bring a flood of waters upon the earth, to destroy all flesh, wherein is the breath of life, from under heaven; and everything that is in the earth shall die.

But with thee will I establish my covenant; and thou shalt come into the ark, thou, and thy sons, and thy wife, and thy sons' wives with thee.

And of every living thing of all flesh, two of every sort shalt thou bring into the ark, to keep them alive with thee; they shall be male and female.

Of fowls after their kind, and of cattle after their kind, of every creeping thing of the earth after his kind, two of every sort shall come unto thee, to keep them alive.

And take thou unto thee of all food that is eaten, and thou shalt gather it to thee; and it shall be for food for thee, and for them.

Thus did Noah; according to all that God commanded him, so did he.

—*Genesis 6:12–22*

Moses: Overcoming Fear and Low Self-Esteem

The great spiritual task facing me is to so fully trust that I belong to God that I can be free in the world—free to speak even when my words are not received; free to act even when my actions are criticized, ridiculed, or considered useless; free also to receive love from people and to be grateful for all the signs of God's presence in the world. I am convinced that I will truly be able to love the world when I fully believe that I am loved far beyond its boundaries.

—*Henri Nouwen*[1]

Now Moses kept the flock of Jethro his father-in-law, the priest of Midian: and he led the flock to the backside of the desert, and came to the mountain of God, even to Horeb.

And the angel of the LORD appeared unto him in a flame of fire out of the midst of a bush: and he looked, and, behold, the bush burned with fire, and the bush was not consumed.

And Moses said, I will now turn aside, and see this great sight, why the bush is not burnt.

And when the LORD saw that he turned aside to see, God called unto him out of the midst of the bush, and said, Moses, Moses. And he said, Here am I.

—Exodus 3:1–4

Moses said unto the people, Fear ye not, stand still, and see the salvation of the LORD, which he will show to you today: for the Egyptians whom ye have seen today, ye shall see them again no more forever.

The LORD shall fight for you, and ye shall hold your peace.

—Exodus 14:13–14

By faith Moses, when he was come to years, refused to be called the son of Pharaoh's daughter;

Choosing rather to suffer affliction with the people of God, than to enjoy the pleasures of sin for a season;

Esteeming the reproach of Christ greater riches than the treasures in Egypt: for he had respect unto the recompense of the reward.

By faith he forsook Egypt, not fearing the wrath of the king: for he endured, as seeing him who is invisible.

Through faith he kept the passover, and the sprinkling of blood, lest he that destroyed the firstborn should touch them.

By faith they passed through the Red sea as by dry land: which the Egyptians assaying to do were drowned.

—Hebrews 11:24–29

Joshua: Courageously Fighting Kingdom Battles

The tenders of vision are often lonely, usually unpopular, and frequently demand that others change. People with a vision inject ambiguity and risk and uncertainty into our lives.

—Max DePree[2]

Now after the death of Moses the servant of the LORD it came to pass, that the LORD spake unto Joshua the son of Nun, Moses' minister, saying,

Moses my servant is dead; now therefore arise, go over this Jordan, thou, and all this people, unto the land which I do give to them, even to the children of Israel.

Every place that the sole of your foot shall tread upon, that have I given unto you, as I said unto Moses.

From the wilderness and this Lebanon even unto the great river, the river Euphrates, all the land of the Hittites, and unto the great sea toward the going down of the sun, shall be your coast.

There shall not any man be able to stand before thee all the days of thy life: as I was with Moses, so I will be with thee: I will not fail thee, nor forsake thee.

Be strong and of a good courage: for unto this people shalt thou divide for an inheritance the land, which I sware unto their fathers to give them.

Only be thou strong and very courageous, that thou mayest observe to do according to all the law, which Moses my servant commanded thee: turn not from it to the right hand or to the left, that thou mayest prosper whithersoever thou goest.

—*Joshua 1:1–9*

Joshua gathered all the tribes of Israel to Shechem, and called for the elders of Israel, and for their heads, and for their judges, and for their officers; and they presented themselves before God.

And Joshua said unto all the people, Thus saith the LORD God of Israel, Your fathers dwelt on the other side of the flood in old time, even Terah, the father of Abraham, and the father of Nachor: and they served other gods. . . .

Now therefore fear the LORD, and serve him in sincerity and in truth: and put away the gods which your fathers served on the other side of the flood, and in Egypt; and serve ye the LORD.

And if it seem evil unto you to serve the LORD, choose you this day whom ye will serve; whether the gods which your fathers served that were on the other side of the flood, or the gods of the Amorites, in whose land ye dwell: but as for me and my house, we will serve the LORD.

—Joshua 24:1–2, 14–15

Joseph: Learning How to Forgive

May I tell you why it seems to me a good thing for us to remember wrong that has been done us? That we may forgive it.

—Charles Dickens

Then Joseph could not refrain himself before all them that stood by him; and he cried, Cause every man to go out from me. And there stood no man with him, while Joseph made himself known unto his brethren.

And he wept aloud: and the Egyptians and the house of Pharaoh heard.

And Joseph said unto his brethren, I am Joseph; doth my father yet live? And his brethren could not answer him; for they were troubled at his presence.

And Joseph said unto his brethren, Come near to me, I pray you. And they came near. And he said, I am Joseph your brother, whom ye sold into Egypt.

Now therefore be not grieved, nor angry with yourselves, that ye sold me hither: for God did send me before you to preserve life.

185

For these two years hath the famine been in the land: and yet there are five years, in the which there shall neither be earing nor harvest.

And God sent me before you to preserve you a posterity in the earth, and to save your lives by a great deliverance.

So now it was not you that sent me hither, but God: and he hath made me a father to Pharaoh, and lord of all his house, and a ruler throughout all the land of Egypt.

Haste ye, and go up to my father, and say unto him, Thus saith thy son Joseph, God hath made me lord of all Egypt: come down unto me, tarry not:

And thou shalt dwell in the land of Goshen, and thou shalt be near unto me, thou, and thy children, and thy children's children, and thy flocks, and thy herds, and all that thou hast:

And there will I nourish thee; for yet there are five years of famine; lest thou, and thy household, and all that thou hast, come to poverty.

And, behold, your eyes see, and the eyes of my brother Benjamin, that it is my mouth that speaketh unto you.

And ye shall tell my father of all my glory in Egypt, and of all that ye have seen; and ye shall haste and bring down my father hither.

And he fell upon his brother Benjamin's neck, and wept; and Benjamin wept upon his neck.

Moreover he kissed all his brethren, and wept upon them: and after that his brethren talked with him.

—*Genesis 45:1–15*

David: Admitting Mistakes

Take heed to yourselves also because there are many eyes upon you. So there will be many who observe your fall. If you miscarry, the world will also echo with it. It is the same as the eclipses of the sun in broad daylight—they are seldom without witnesses.

—*Richard Baxter*

The LORD sent Nathan unto David. And he came unto him, and said unto him, There were two men in one city; the one rich, and the other poor.

The rich man had exceeding many flocks and herds:

But the poor man had nothing, save one little ewe lamb, which he had bought and nourished up: and it grew up together with him, and with his children; it did eat of his own meat, and drank of his own cup, and lay in his bosom, and was unto him as a daughter.

And there came a traveler unto the rich man, and he spared to take of his own flock and of his own herd, to dress for the wayfaring man that was come unto him; but took the poor man's lamb, and dressed it for the man that was come to him.

And David's anger was greatly kindled against the man; and he said to Nathan, As the LORD liveth, the man that hath done this thing shall surely die:

And he shall restore the lamb fourfold, because he did this thing, and because he had no pity.

And Nathan said to David, Thou art the man. Thus saith the LORD God of Israel, I anointed thee king over Israel, and I delivered thee out of the hand of Saul;

And I gave thee thy master's house, and thy master's wives into thy bosom, and gave thee the house of Israel and of Judah; and if that had been too little, I would moreover have given unto thee such and such things.

Wherefore hast thou despised the commandment of the LORD, to do evil in his sight? thou hast killed Uriah the Hittite with the sword, and hast taken his wife to be thy wife, and hast slain him with the sword of the children of Ammon.

Now therefore the sword shall never depart from thine house; because thou hast despised me, and hast taken the wife of Uriah the Hittite to be thy wife.

Thus saith the LORD, Behold, I will raise up evil against thee out of thine own house, and I will take thy wives before thine eyes, and give them unto thy neighbor, and he shall lie with thy wives in the sight of this sun.

For thou didst it secretly: but I will do this thing before all Israel, and before the sun.

And David said unto Nathan, I have sinned against the LORD.

—2 Samuel 12:1–13a

Paul: Pursuing Christian Maturity

The progress of our spiritual growth is not a matter of our own initiative and designing; it is under the control and direction of God who has begun a good work in us and will work patiently to perfect it until the day of Christ.

—*Richard F. Lovelace*[3]

Be ye followers of me, even as I also am of Christ.

1 Corinthians 11:1

When he had received meat, he was strengthened. Then was Saul certain days with the disciples which were at Damascus.

And straightway he preached Christ in the synagogues, that he is the Son of God.

But all that heard him were amazed, and said; Is not this he that destroyed them which called on this name in Jerusalem, and came hither for that intent, that he might bring them bound unto the chief priests?

But Saul increased the more in strength, and confounded the Jews which dwelt at Damascus, proving that this is very Christ.

—*Acts 9:19–22*

There is therefore now no condemnation to them which are in Christ Jesus, who walk not after the flesh, but after the Spirit.

—*Romans 8:1*

Not as though I had already attained, either were already perfect: but I follow after, if that I may apprehend that for which also I am apprehended of Christ Jesus.

Brethren, I count not myself to have apprehended: but this one thing I do, forgetting those things which are behind, and reaching forth unto those things which are before,

I press toward the mark for the prize of the high calling of God in Christ Jesus.

Let us therefore, as many as be perfect, be thus minded: and if in anything ye be otherwise minded, God shall reveal even this unto you.

Nevertheless, whereto we have already attained, let us walk by the same rule, let us mind the same thing.

Brethren, be followers together of me, and mark them which walk so as ye have us for an example.

—Philippians 3:12–17

Jesus: Becoming a Servant-Leader

In only three years Christ defined a mission and formed strategies to carry it out. With a staff of twelve unlikely men, He organized Christianity, which today has branches in all the world's countries and a 32.4 percent share of the world's population, twice as big as its nearest rival. Managers want to develop people to their full potential, taking ordinary people and making them extraordinary. This is what Christ did with His disciples. Jesus was the most effective executive in history. The results He achieved are second to none.

—James Hind[4]

Ye call me Master and Lord: and ye say well; for so I am.

If I then, your Lord and Master, have washed your feet; ye also ought to wash one another's feet.

—*John 13:13–14*

Let this mind be in you, which was also in Christ Jesus:

Who, being in the form of God, thought it not robbery to be equal with God:

But made himself of no reputation, and took upon him the form of a servant, and was made in the likeness of men:

And being found in fashion as a man, he humbled himself, and became obedient unto death, even the death of the cross.

Wherefore God also hath highly exalted him, and given him a name which is above every name:

That at the name of Jesus every knee should bow, of things in heaven, and things in earth, and things under the earth;

And that every tongue should confess that Jesus Christ is Lord, to the glory of God the Father.

—*Philippians 2:5–11*

For even hereunto were ye called: because Christ also suffered for us, leaving us an example, that ye should follow his steps:

Who did no sin, neither was guile found in his mouth:

Who, when he was reviled, reviled not again; when he suffered, he threatened not; but committed himself to him that judgeth righteously:

Who his own self bare our sins in his own body on the tree, that we, being dead to sins, should live unto righteousness: by whose stripes ye were healed.

For ye were as sheep going astray; but are now returned unto the Shepherd and Bishop of your souls.

—*1 Peter 2:21–25*

Notes

—Chapter One—

1 Gerald May, *The Awakened Heart* (San Francisco: Harper Collins, 1988).

2 Marlon Brando, in *Chicago Tribune Magazine,* 20 November 1994.

—Chapter Two—

1 William Bennett, in *The Book of Virtues* (New York: Simon and Schuster, 1993), quoted in *Reader's Digest* (February 1996).

2 Paul Tournier, quoted in *Quote Unquote* (Wheaton: Victor Books).

3 W. Phillip Keller, quoted in the *Men's Devotional Bible* (Grand Rapids: Zondervan, 1993).

—Chapter Three—

1 C. S. Lewis, *Mere Christianity* (New York: Macmillan, 1971).

2 Gerald May, *The Awakened Heart* (San Francisco: Harper & Row, 1991).

3 Dag Hammarskjold, in *The HarperCollins Book of Prayers* Robert Van deWeyer, ed. (San Francisco: HarperSanFrancisco, 1993).

4 Henri Nouwen, Ibid.

—Chapter Four—

1 Deitrich Bonhoeffer, *Life Together* (San Fransisco: Harper & Row, 1954).

2 E. Paul Hovey, in *The Treasury of Inspirational Anecdotes, Quotations, and Illustrations,* E. Paul Hovey, comp. (Grand Rapids: Revell, 1987).

—Chapter Five—

1 Allan Nevins, quoted in *Treasury of Inspiriational Anecdotes, Quotations, and Illustrations,* E. Paul Hovey, comp. (Grand Rapids: Revell, 1987).

—Chapter Six—

1 James Houston, quoted in Paul Stanley and J. Robert Clinton, *Connecting* (Colorado Springs: NavPress, 1992).

2 Stan and Jan Berenstain quoted in *Readers Digest* (March 1996).

3 Patrick Morley, *Walking with Christ in the Details of Life* (Thomas Nelson), as quoted in *New Man Magazine* (March–April 1995).

—Chapter Seven—

1 Donald T. Kauffman, *Gist of the Lesson.*

2 H. Norman Wright, *Seasons of a Marriage* (Ventura, Calif.: Regal Books, 1983).

3 Peter Ustinov, in "Points to Ponder," *Reader's Digest,* (October 1992).

4 James B. Nelson, *The Intimate Connection* (Philadelphia: Westminster Press, 1988).

—Chapter Eight—

1 Cecil Osborne, in *The Art of Learning to Love Yourself.*

—Chapter Nine—

1 Toki Miyashina, in *The Complete Book of Christian Prayer* (New York: Continuum, 1995).

—Chapter Ten—

1 Henri Nouwen, "Beyond the Mirror," in *Christianity Today* (29 April 1991).

2 Max DePree, *Leadership Jazz* (New York: Dell, 1992).

3 Richard F. Lovelace, *Dynamics of the Spiritual Life: An Evangelical Theology of Renewal* (Downers Grove: InterVarsity Press, 1979), 118.

4 James Hind, in the December issue of *Life* (quoted in *New Man Magazine,* March—April 1995).